THE BEE PEOPLE

THE BEE PEOPLE

BY

MARGARET WARNER MORLEY

Illustrated by the author

YESTERDAY'S CLASSICS
CHAPEL HILL, NORTH CAROLINA

This edition, first published in 2009 by Yesterday's Classics, an imprint of Yesterday's Classics, LLC, is an unabridged republication of the text originally published by A. C. McClurg & Company in 1914. For the complete listing of the books that are published by Yesterday's Classics, please visit www.yesterdaysclassics.com. Yesterday's Classics is the publishing arm of the Baldwin Online Children's Literature Project which presents the complete text of hundreds of classic books for children at www.mainlesson.com.

ISBN-10: 1-59915-318-1

ISBN-13: 978-1-59915-318-6

Yesterday's Classics, LLC
PO Box 3418
Chapel Hill, NC 27515

CONTENTS

INTRODUCTION

BEES and flowers belong together. We cannot understand the one without the other. For, you see, bees get their food from the flowers, and the flowers need the bees to enable them to form their seeds.

The flowers that we like best have bright-colored petals. The petals of a rose are pink or white or yellow. The petals of a violet are purple, and those of a forget-me-not are blue.

Sometimes the petals are separate, as in a rose or a buttercup, and you can pull them off one by one.

Sometimes they are all grown into one piece, like the funnel-shaped flower of the morning-glory.

The Wild Rose with five separate petals

The Morning-Glory with the petals grown together into a funnel

The bees can see the bright colors of the flowers a long way off. The can also smell them, for bright flowers are generally fragrant.

Flowers make a sweet juice on purpose to feed bees and other insects. We call this sweet juice nectar, and the bees take it home and make honey of it.

The flowers like to have the bees come and take the nectar. Why, do you suppose? If you have studied flowers, you will know; if you have not, I must try to tell you.

You know there is a yellow dust in some flowers. It gets on your face when you smell of them. Sometimes flower dust is brown and sometimes it is white. If you shake a golden-rod in the fall, a cloud of yellow golden-rod dust will fly out. This dust is called pollen.

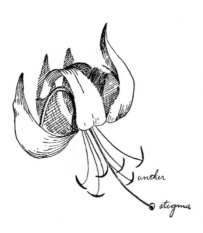

anther

stigma

Nearly all flowers have it. It grows in little boxes called anthers; and when the anthers are ripe; they burst open and let out the pollen.

You know how the anthers in a lily look. They swing on the ends of the six long slender stems that stick out of the lily flower.

Nearly all flowers have anthers, but some do not have stems to the anthers. Sometimes the anthers grow right against the inside of the flowers, but wherever they may be they *always* contain pollen.

In the centre of the flower is another part that looks a little like an anther; its stem is long, and it is marked *stigma* in the picture. This stigma is not filled with pollen. It is just a sticky knob.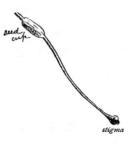

When it gets ripe it gets sticky. If any pollen touches it, the pollen sticks fast. If you take away the petals and the anthers and their stems from the lily, this is what you will have left.

You see it is the stigma and its long stem, and there is another knob at the other end of the stem opposite the stigma. This other knob is hollow. It is a seed-cup and is filled with seeds. The seeds cannot grow without pollen.

If the pollen gets on the stigma, then all goes well. The sticky stigma holds it fast. It finds its way down through the long stem to the little seeds. It nourishes them, and they grow. But if the pollen does not come, the seeds die.

Flowers do not like their own pollen. One lily prefers the pollen from another lily.

It is better for the seeds. But how to get this pollen?

Why, the hairy-coated bees bring it, to be sure.

And now you see why the flower makes nectar.

It wishes to coax the bees to come. When the bees go down to the bottom of the flower after nectar, they will be sure to get their coats dusty with pollen. Then they fly to anther flower, and some of the pollen on their coats is rubbed against the stigma and stuck fast there.

The nectar is always placed so that the bees have to touch the anthers and the stigma of the flower on their way to the feast.

Many flowers have bright lines or spots leading to the nectar that the bee may lose no time in finding it. These are called nectar guides, and you can see them very plainly in the morning-glory.

Many other insects besides bees visit flowers. Butterflies and moths and flies and even some beetles are fond of nectar and pollen, and they all carry pollen about from plant to plant.

When insects carry pollen to the stigmas, we say they *fertilize* the flowers. Unless a flower is fertilized, it will bear no seed.

Bees eat pollen as well as honey, and while gathering it from different flowers they are sure to dust the stigmas.

Flowers can be fertilized only by pollen from other flowers of their own kind. Lilies can be fertilized only by pollen from other lilies, and roses by the pollen of other roses. Lily pollen cannot fertilize a rose, nor can any pollen fertilize any flower but one of its own particular kind. The three chief parts of a bee are the head, the thorax, and the abdomen.

The head bears the antennæ, tongue, and eyes.

The thorax has attached to it the wings and legs. In the abdomen are the sting and the honey-sac.

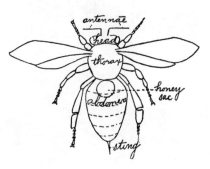

APIS MELLIFICA, OR
THE HONEY-BEE

THE honey-bees are buzzy, fuzzy little pepper-pots.

They have pretty, shining wings, but if you so much as touch one of them you will see what happens!

You cannot wonder that they do not like to have you come too near, for they are such little creatures that even a small child must seem to them a tremendous giant.

How would you like to see a great warm creature as large as a hill come lumbering up and try to put a finger the size of a church steeple upon you?

I am sure you would do anything to keep it away, and if you had a good sharp sting you would use it. So we must not blame the Bee People for stinging us.

It is the only way they have of telling us to keep away and let them alone.

They are friendly enough to their own relations, as

you will agree when you learn that there are sometimes as many as sixty thousand of them living happily together in one family.

Sometimes we build houses, which we call hives, for them, and sometimes they live in a hollow tree in the woods.

Modern Hives

The hives we usually make in these days are square-cornered boxes that can be opened to take out the honey or to attend to the bees. In some parts of the country an old-fashioned hive called a "bee gum" is still used. If you go to the mountains of North Carolina, you will

Bee Gums

see a great many bee gums. Nearly every cabin has a row of them in its yard, and they are made by chopping down hollow sweet-gum trees and cutting off lengths of about three feet.

Sometimes other hollow trees are used, but they are all called "gums." The mountaineers stand the "gum" on a board or a stone, and put anther board or stone on top for a roof. All the holes are plastered up with mud except those near the bottom, where the bees go in and out. The mud is used to keep out moths, which otherwise might get in and spoil the honey-combs.

A row of bee gums standing beside a log cabin on a mountain-side is very pretty.

A skep is a hive made of twisted straw, and in old times was used more than any other, particularly in England. It had a peculiar shape,

Skeps

and to this day when we say a thing is hive-shaped, we mean it is shaped like the skep.

Once in a while honey-bees make their home in the hollow walls of a building, and there is a house in a New England city where bees have lived for a number of years. They are under the roof somewhere, and there they stay safe, and year after year store up honey which nobody can reach. Stories are told of old houses whose hollow walls, when they were pulled down, were found to be filled with honey-combs. It is not easy to get honey that is stored in the walls of houses, as the bees fight bravely for their property.

Honey-bees are small people, being only about twice as large as common house-flies.

Some are brown all over, and some that were brought here from Italy have tan-colored abdomens, but all of them, the brown bees, the Italian bees, and the other kinds of hive bees in this country, are called by the same name, *Apis Mellifica*. *Apis* is the Latin word for bee, and *mellifica* is the Latin word for honey-making; and they have this pretty name because they make and store up quantities of good honey, which we like to eat.

The Bee People are sun-lovers, and all summer long on bright days you may see them hurrying about. But in the winter-time you would look in vain for them, no matter how brightly the sun might shine, for they are

White Clover, from which a great deal of honey is made

4

Friends of the Flowers and seldom leave home except when there are blossoms for them to visit.

Many flowers keep a dainty table spread for the bees. Cups of nectar and dishes of ambrosia are ready for them to eat and drink and carry home.

If it were not for these gifts from the flowers, the honey-bees could not live, as they get all their food from their flower friends.

APIS MELLIFICA AND HER EYES

H ERE comes a little brown lady whose name is
Apis Mellifica. She is making her wings go so fast
that they buzz like a humming-top. Straight as an arrow
she goes to that morning-glory flower. All at once the
buzzing stops; little Miss Apis has landed feet
down and right side up on the nectar guide.

Such great eyes as stare at you when you
look her full in the face! No wonder she saw
the bright flower a long way off and came
straight to it.

She has more eye-space for her
size than an owl, which is saying
a good deal. In fact,
her head looks as
if it were nearly
all eyes,—for two
large ones cover
the sides.
And if you
will believe

me, in the space between the two large eyes, right on top of her heard, are three small ones!

Unless you shave Miss Apis's head you can see but one of these small eyes at a time, as there is a tuft of hairs in front of each, which hides it unless you are looking right down into it. In the picture Miss Apis's head has been shaved.

Miss Apis's face

Five eyes!

But that is not all. Each of her two large eyes is made up of about six thousand three hundred *very* small ones.

Really, Miss Apis, twelve thousand six hundred and three eyes are a goodly supply for one bee.

It is fortunate that she does not have to keep count of them, for if she counted an eye every second it would take almost four hours to get to the end, without stopping to take a sip of honey, or even to say, Oh, dear me!

How would you like your mother to look at you out of more than twelve thousand eyes when you had been doing something naughty? Two eyes are bad enough at such times. Let us hope that young bees never do wrong.

Just imagine a naughty little bee looking up to find twelve thousand six hundred small eyes and three large ones solemnly staring at his wickedness!

The truth is, all the thousands of small eyes that

make up each large eye work together and act as one large eye.

Miss Apis's large eyes are called "compound eyes" because they are made of so many small eyes, or "facets."

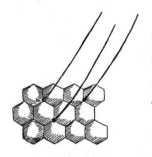 The facets are so very small that you cannot see them except by the aid of a microscope; and here is a picture showing you a portion of the eye considerably magnified.

Whoever goes as far as Miss Apis does in search of flowers needs good eyes that can see a long distance. She has been known to fly four or five miles in search of flowers; just think of going back and forth from hive to flowers and flowers to hive any such distance as that! As a rule, however, Miss Apis goes only a little way, half a mile or so, but even for this she needs good, far-seeing eyes.

And she has them,—for her compound eyes are very far-sighted.

This is probably the reason she needs the three small eyes, which are near-sighted and enable her to see things close at hand.

Although she possesses such a prodigious number of eyes, Miss Apis has no eyelids. No, indeed! She has eye-hairs instead, that point outward and do not prevent her seeing but keep dust and pollen from getting into her eyes.

If you look back at the picture of the facets, you

will see some of these hairs. She combs her eyes every time she combs her head, and this does not seem at all funny to her, for, you see, she is used to it.

Wild Grape

HER TONGUE

M EANTIME, while we have been gossiping about Miss Apis's eyes, she has gone off.

There she is, just landing in another morning-glory blossom. She strikes the nectar guide as a shot strikes the bull's eye, then down she tumbles to the very bottom of the flower. Here are the nectar cups, five of them, filled full of sweet clear nectar, for it is early in the morning, and Miss Apis is the first to arrive. She wants this nectar to carry home and make into honey, but how is she going to get her head into the tiny openings that lead to the nectar?

You need not worry about that. She knows what to do, and all at once produces a long shining brown tongue and thrusts it deep down into her nectar.

Here is a morning-glory that must have had an X-ray turned upon it, for we can see right through it to where Miss Apis is reaching her brown tongue down to the nectar.

This tongue is almost as queer as her eyes. Not that she has twelve thousand six hundred tongues. Oh, no; one tongue like hers is quite enough, as you probably will agree when you know more about it.

It is a long tongue and a strong tongue, and curls about, lapping up the sweetness, as you can see for yourself if you catch her and give her a drop of honey.

But now she has licked the morning-glory dry and—but what *has* she done with her tongue?

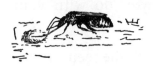

Enjoying a drop of honey

It was almost as long as her body a moment ago, and now it is gone.

Miss Apis, what have you done with your tongue?

Where is your tongue, Miss Apis?

MISS APIS, MISS APIS! YOUR TONGUE, MISS APIS?

But she only looks at us out of her twelve thousand

six hundred large eyes and her three small eyes, and says not a word.

Her tongue is all right, and she knows how to hold it.

There, she is going to speak! Buzz—b-u-z-z-zz. No, that is her wing music; her tongue is still silent. Off she goes and leaves us in despair concerning it. Now she has deposited herself in another flower—and sure enough—yes—there is that l-o-n-g, b-r-o-w-n tongue wriggling around in the nectar cup.

I will catch hold of it and pull it, Miss Apis, if you do not tell me what you did with it.

Will you? she seems to say, solemnly looking at us out of her twelve thousand six hundred and three eyes.

No, we will not, because it is gone again.

I think, in spite of her solemn and owl-like looks, she is laughing at us.

Saucy Miss Apis, what *do* you do with your tongue?

"I know what you do with yours," she seems to say, and flies off.

But now I know. I saw her do it. She pulled it in, just as you do yours when you have put it out of your mouth. But hers is such a large tongue it could not be pulled into her mouth at all.. The best she could do was to pull it up as short as possible, and then fold it back into a nice little groove under her head.

12

It is a very useful tongue and a very queer one. It has to reach down into long flower-cups, and so it must be long. It has to lap up honey, and so it must be flexible. It has to find its way though very small openings, and so it must be as slender as a thread.

It often has to come into contact with the hard parts of flowers and plants, and so it must be protected.

It is protected by two hard horny sheaths,—one covering the upper side of the tongue, (T); the other covering the lower side. The lower sheath is made of two long pieces, X, X, that can be separated, as you see in the picture. Each has a little feeler F at the end. Usually they lie side by side with their edges over-lapping underneath the tongue. They make a little trough in which the tongue lies, as you see in this next picture. They protect the under side of the tongue.

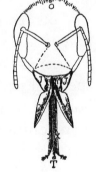

The upper sheath is also made of two horny pieces Y, Y that can be separated from each other. They lie side by side when not separated, and their inner edges overlap so that they form a covering to the upper side of the tongue. So, you see, when the two sheaths are in their right places they make a tube about the tongue, and the tongue is run out at the point of the sheaths when the bee wants to lick up nectar.

Miss Apis has her tongue-sheath separated into so many parts for a very good reason.

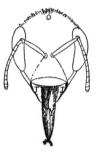

If the sheath were a closed tube, pieces of honey-comb or grains of pollen or other substances might get wedged in, when she was licking up honey or nectar, and give her a great deal of trouble. But as it is, if anything gets caught, all she has to do is to separate the parts of her tongue-sheath and clear it out.

Miss Apis's tongue is surrounded by rings of hairs which hold fast the nectar and enable her to draw it up into her mouth through the tube made by her tongue-sheaths.

The very tip of her tongue is like a little round plate and helps her to lick up the honey.

You see by now that Miss Apis's tongue is a very sweet tongue, in fact, a honeyed tongue, as we might say. We speak of poets and orators as having honeyed tongues, but I leave it to you if any of them can equal Miss Apis in this.

If you look in Miss Apis's face when she is not eating, you cannot see her tongue at all, as it is folded back under her head.

You can see her tightly closed jaws, J, J and her upper lip, but not her tongue.

Here she has opened her jaws and let her tongue down between them, but you can see only the upper sheath and the two little feelers that grow on the points of the lower sheath.

In this next picture she has pushed her tongue out below the sheaths, as she does when licking up honey or nectar that is easily reached.

If the nectar is hard to get at she needs a longer tongue, and therefore shoots the under sheath out below the upper one.

When she does this her tongue is not so well protected, but it is longer, as you can see in this next picture.

When the tongue is not in use, it is drawn up as short as possible, and then is folded back into a groove on the under-side of Miss Apis's head, something as a boy shuts his knife-blade into the handle.

Side view of Miss Apis's head with the tongue (T) folded back

Getting honey is very easy where it is in open cups, but sometimes the flower sweets are in the bottoms of the tubes too long for the bee's tongue to reach them.

What is she to do in such a case? When she smells a delicious meal which she cannot reach, shall she pass by with a sigh because she cannot get it? Sometimes she is obliged to, but sometimes she is helped by the bumble-bees.

These are much larger than honey-bees; and you will know them because they are covered all over with hair, as if they had on furry coats. Honey-bees have very little hair on the body below the waist. Bumble-bees have broad bands of yellow hairs across their bodies, and sometimes the whole thorax, or part between the

head and waist, is bright yellow. Bumble-bees can always be found in red clover fields. Their horny tongue-sheaths are larger and stronger than the sheaths of the honey bee. Indeed, they make quite

Madam Bombus,
the Bumble-Bee

a strong little dagger with which Madam Bombus, the bumble-bee, can cut a hole in a flower.

When Madam Bombus finds a flower with sweets which she cannot reach without taking too much trouble, she goes to the spot beneath which the sweet she wants is concealed, and, with a downward blow of her convenient dagger, rips open the intervening membrane. Then she unfurls her flag in triumph. In this case her flag is her tongue, you understand. She inserts it in the hole she has made and licks out the sweet juice.

After she is gone, comes the turn of Miss Apis, who

puts her tongue through the hole that her larger and stronger friend has made, and takes her share also.

Since the nectaries of the flowers usually fill up as soon as the bees have licked them out, Miss Apis may get as much honey as though Madam Bombus had not taken any.

So you see that the bees help each other to get at their food. But I do not think Miss Honey-Bee knows who has cut open the flowers for her.

The tidy little Touch-me-not

It is the flowers with spurs that Madam Bombus most often cuts into in this ungracious manner. I myself have seen her go up to a tidy little touch-me-not cup, and passing straight by the open door in front, cling to the yellow spur at the back, which holds the nectar, and with no hesitation whatever thrust her sharp little dagger into the spur, slit a hole there, and take out the nectar.

It is difficult to believe this of a very respectable-looking being with several thousands of solemn eyes that make her look many times as wise as an owl, but it only proves how little one can rely upon appearances in this world.

It seems to be unwise for Madam Bombus to do such a thing; for by going in at the front door she would preserve the lives of the flowers that feed her.

When she goes about slitting open nectaries, she injures not only herself but all her fellow-bees; for bees carry pollen from flower to flower, as you very well know, and this pollen is necessary to the forming of the seeds. When the bees go into a flower as they ought, they carry some of the pollen that has rubbed off against their hairy bodies to the next flower they visit, which is just what the flowers need. But when they break open the nectaries from the outside, they do not get dusted with pollen, and do not carry it to other flowers. No pollen, no seeds; no seeds, no more plants; so now you understand why the bees do harm when they cut nectaries open.

The honey-bees seldom do this, because they cannot. Their dagger sheath is not strong enough. I once saw a

Purple Azaleas

honey-bee try very hard to cut a hole in the long tube of a purple azalea. She could not reach the nectar from the front of the flower, because the tube was too long and slender, so she tried to break in the back way. But she could not do it, and all the azalea nectar she got she sucked out of holes which the bumble bees had made in some of the flowers. The azalea did not make honey for the bees; its long and slender tube was fitted to the tongues of large moths and butterflies.

HER HONEY-SAC

W HAT do you suppose becomes of the nectar Miss Apis gathers with her hairy tongue? She swallows it, you say, and that is true. She *does* swallow it, but that is not the end of the story. When it is swallowed,  it passes into a little honey-sac which is not as large as a sweet-pea seed, and which is so delicate that it looks like a little soap bubble.

This honey-sac is in the big end of the abdomen, and in the picture it is shown by a dotted circle. It holds less than a drop of nectar, and we may call it the jug or bottle in which Miss Apis carries the blossom nectar home; for she does not swallow it for her own use, but that she may bear it to the hive for the baby bees to eat.

You can see this honey-sac by feeding a hive bee as much as she wants, and then letting her fly to the window. The light shining through the delicate body makes the clear honey in her little "bottle" plainly visible. The Italian honey-bees, whose abdomens are a light tan color, at the upper end, show the honey-drop better than the common brown bees.

Some of the honey passes on into the true stomach of the bee, which is just beyond the honey-sac, and is digested; but the most of it Miss Apis carries to the hive in her honey-sac.

It is curious that everything Miss Apis eats has to be swallowed into the honey-sac before it can get into the stomach, and yet the honey is always clear and pure. Honey and pollen go together into the honey-sac, yet the honey in the comb contains almost no pollen.

The reason is, Miss Apis *strains* her honey before she puts it into the comb.

In her honey-sac is a little strainer which is very wonderful and very beautiful.

It looks, as you can see in the picture, something like a flower-bud.  Honey and pollen grains go together into the honey-sac, but they do not stay together, for the pollen grains are gathered up by the action of muscles in the walls of the honey-sac, and passed through the strainer into the stomach. The strainer opens its mouth to let them pass, but as soon as they have done so, it closes. Of course a good deal of nectar passes through with the pollen, but this is squeezed back by the muscles of the stomach into the honey-sac through the closed mouth of the strainer. The mouth of the strainer is fringed with hairs that point backwards and cross each other when the strainer mouth is closed. So, though the nectar can squeeze through, the pollen grains cannot. They are kept back in the stomach by this clever little strainer, and only pure nectar or honey can get back into the honey-sac.

When Miss Apis gets to the hive, she makes the muscles of her honey-sac squeeze the honey into her mouth, and she then puts it into the honey-comb.

Miss Apis swallows nectar, as the sweet juice of the flowers is called, but when we take honey from the honey-comb, it has undergone a change and is no longer nectar, but honey. In some way the nectar has been changed and made into honey.

Wild Raspberry

AMBROSIA AND NECTAR

O F course no one, not even Miss Apis nor the lovely Venus herself, could live entirely upon nectar.

We know that the gods and goddesses, when they had a party on Mount Olympus, always had ambrosia as well as nectar.

They sat around and had it passed to them by the graceful goddess Hebe. She was as beautiful as the springtime, and I have no doubt they often ate and drank more than was good for them, just for the sake of having her bring them one more cup of nectar or one more slice of ambrosia.

The nectar of the gods was like honey; some say that nine-tenths of it was honey.

Just what ambrosia was, I am not able to say, but I suppose it was like the best bread that ever was made on earth, only a great deal better; and like the most delicious cake that ever was concocted for Christmas time, only a great deal more delicious; and like all the bonbons and good things rolled into one, only a great deal sweeter and finer than anything we can possibly imagine.

Miss Apis, too, takes ambrosia with her nectar, though hers is not at all like that of the gods and goddesses. She gets it from the flowers, and is very fond of it. Though we do not agree with her concerning the excellence of her feast. But then we might not like the ambrosia the gods were fond of. Tastes differ. Her ambrosia just suits Miss Apis. In fact, she finds it so much to her mind that she seldom eats anything else. She drinks nectar and eats ambrosia. Her nectar is the sweet juice of the flowers, and her ambrosia is the pollen of the flowers,—a very precious ambrosia indeed.

Miss Apis not only eats all she wants when she visits the flowers, but she mixes nectar and pollen together and carries them away with her.

She is able to do this for she *always* carries baskets on purpose. She never yet was known to go away from home and forget to take her pollen baskets.

MISS APIS'S LEGS

THE reason Miss Apis never forgets her baskets is, that they are fastened on to her. For, I must tell you, her legs are as remarkable as her twelve thousand six hundred and three eyes, her folding tongue, and her very peculiar honey-sac.

She has six legs fastened to her thorax, which you remember is the division of her body next back of her head.

Although she is so well supplied with legs, she has no arms; since she has no arms, she has no hands.

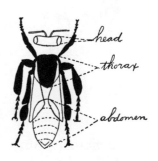

That seems rather unfortunate, and we are inclined to be sorry for her, but I doubt she would thank us for feeling so.

She probably feels sorry for us because we have not six legs, and wonders how we get along with only two to prop us up and help us to go about, with not even wings to help. For besides six legs, Miss Apis has four wings. They are wonderful wings; but we must return to legs.

Since Miss Apis has no hands, she uses all six legs, or rather the claws at the ends of them, for clinging fast to things.

She also uses all six legs to walk and run with, and once in a while, when under great excitement, to jump a little.

The claws at the ends of her legs are not ordinary claws such as cats or hens have; there is nothing ordinary about Miss Apis, I must remind you, not even her claws.

In this picture you can see Miss Apis's foot and the claw at the end very plainly.

The truth is, she has been sitting with her foot under the microscope, and if you will believe me, picture number II. is just what you see in the circle in picture number I., only number II. is very much magnified.

The claw at the end, as you see in the picture number II., is made of four sharp points, two long and two short ones.

There is a claw like this at the end of each of Miss Apis's six feet.

They are as good as a whole box of tools, being a great deal better than hands and fingers for doing some of the things she is in the habit of doing. Between the points on each foot is a small pad (+), that can stick fast to smooth surfaces like the pad on a fly's foot, and so enable Miss Apis to walk on slippery places if she wants to.

Her foot is made of four very movable joints besides the claw, and this enables her to curl it about objects so as to get a better grasp of them.

When she pleases she can turn up her claws and use them as hooks by which to suspend herself. You will see later that it is very important for her to be able to hang herself up when she wishes.

But what have her legs to do with pollen baskets? you are asking.

They have a great deal to do with them, for Miss Apis carries her baskets on her hind legs.

Oh, well, laugh if you want to. I have known people before who laughed too soon.

I wonder where *you* would fit pollen baskets to Miss Apis if you had it to do?

Probably you would put them on her head, where she could not see because of them, and where she could

27

not reach them, and where the pollen would always be spilling out, if she ever succeeded in getting any in.

But I can tell you, you might look Miss Apis over from top to toe, and you would not find another place as good as her hind legs for disposing of pollen baskets.

Each of her legs has ten joints. There are two small ones (1, 2) close to the body, which are very much alike on all the legs. Then comes a long joint (3) which is quite similar in all six legs; then comes a second long joint (4) which is very curious.

The fifth joint is also interesting. 6, 7, 8, 9 are the small joints forming the foot, and 10 is the last joint of all, or the claw.

Miss Apis carries her pollen baskets on the outside of the fourth joint of each of her hind legs. As she walks about, they are not in her way. She does not spill the pollen, and she can easily reach the baskets with her other legs when she wants to fill them.

The outside of the joint is hollowed a little, and along the outer edge of this hollow space are stiff hairs that turn towards the middle and make a very complete little basket to hold the pollen that is put into it.

Miss Apis has been kind enough to sit with her left hind leg under the microscope and have its picture taken, so we can see the pollen basket very clearly.

The large leg at the left of Miss Apis is the magnified picture of the leg in the circle.

If you look at her with a little hand-magnifying glass, you can get quite a good view of her pollen baskets.

How do you suppose Miss Apis gets the pollen which she puts into her baskets?

If you look at her body and at the upper part of all her six legs, you will find them covered with long hairs. If you look at the hairs under a magnifying glass you will find them branched, as you see in the picture.

When Miss Apis wants pollen she scrapes it from the anther cells with her claws, and gathers it together with her leg. Very often her whole body becomes dusted with it, and wherever the pollen grains touch the branched hairs they cling fast to them. Miss Apis wriggles about in the flowers, scraping out the pollen with her feet, and collecting it on her branched hairs. Then she carefully brushes it together, and by means of her legs transfers it to her pollen baskets.

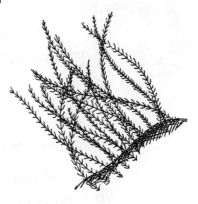

For you must know she has a number of brushes on her legs to help her to gather up the pollen.

These brushes are tufts or rows of stiff hairs that are not branched.

If we look on the *under* side of her hind leg, the

same that bears the pollen basket on the fourth joint of its *upper* side, we shall see two kinds of brushes or

combs for gathering the pollen together, the stiff hairs on the edge of the fourth joint, and the sharp teeth that cover the fifth joint. 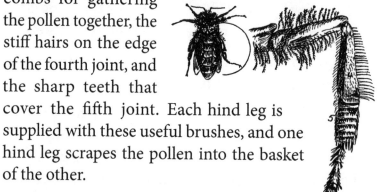 Each hind leg is supplied with these useful brushes, and one hind leg scrapes the pollen into the basket of the other.

The first chance you get you must watch Miss Apis gathering pollen. Sometimes she looks as if she were running about over a head of flowers to find something she had lost,—now this way and now that she goes in a great hurry, then turns around and around. But she has not lost anything, and she has not gone crazy; she is merely collecting pollen as fast as she can, and if you have sharp eyes you will see her rub, rub, rubbing it with her legs back into her baskets.

Full pollen basket

It is astonishing how much she can carry. When her baskets are full she goes about with a ball of pollen attached to each of her hind legs.

If she goes into morning-glory blossoms, this pollen

30

ball is white; if she happens to be visiting wood-lilies, it is dark reddish brown; and if she has been going to see the sweet-peas, it is bright yellow. She carries it to the hive and stores it up there for the young bees and for winter use, and it soon assumes a uniform dark brown color.

There is nothing neater than a bee. It disturbs her terribly to have a dirty face or a dusty wing, and she is forever cleaning herself.

If you look along the outer edge of the fifth joint on her front leg, you will see her eye-comb. She has to keep the pollen and dust combed out of her eye-hairs —or else how could she see? And when she is combing her eyes she evidently thinks she may just as well, being a very neat person, comb her head also.

She cleans off her velvety thorax with the brushes on her middle legs, where she also carries a prong for preening her wings, and for prying the pollen out of her baskets. You can see this prong on the inside of her middle leg at the bottom of the fourth joint. You see the pollen is really the flour from which she makes her bee bread, or ambrosia, as it is sometimes

her prong

called. As she collects it she moistens it with honey so that it can be kneaded into a sticky mass, like dough, and thus packed securely in her baskets.

31

All her legs have brushes, and when she is pollen-gathering you can see her dusting every part of her body with these brushes.

Over her head she passes the brushes on her fore legs, over her back and under her body she passes the brushes on her middle legs.

Then she rubs her legs together to collect the pollen on the combs of the hind legs.

Since she gathers the flour for her bread on the hair of her body, she is obliged to keep herself very, very clean, so all the leg brushes are also toilet brushes, and are used to keep her clean as well as to gather pollen.

The most remarkable of her toilet articles are her antenna cleaners, but their story comes later.

It is much easier to watch Miss Apis performing her toilet than it is to distinguish her various combs and brushes. If you wet her a little, then dust her lightly with flour and put her on the window, you can see the whole operation.

She generally cleans her antennæ, and combs her head and eyes first. She turns her head from side to side, and puts her front leg up over it and draws her convenient comb through the hairs. She turns her head about, using first one front leg and then the other, until she has it as clean as a bee's head ought to be. She generally puts out her tongue and gives that a good rubbing too, grasping it in both her fore feet.

When you watch a bee performing her toilet you will understand why her legs are so beautifully jointed. She must be able to move them in all directions, and put them over her back or under her body.

She generally cleans her back with her middle legs; and her abdomen, as the last division of the body is called, with her hind legs.

She also uses her hind legs to clean her wings, drawing down one wing at a time and holding it tightly against her side while she polishes it with her brushes.

She spends a great deal of time rubbing her hind legs together, and sometimes she performs the difficult acrobatic feat of standing on her two front legs and rubbing the other four together.

She looks very cunning as she rubs and scrubs every part of her fuzzy little body; and if you want to see her do it, all you need do is to look.

No matter how dirty she may have become, if she is allowed to stand still for a few minutes she will look as if she had on a new suit of clothes and had never known what it was to touch a speck of dirt; so effective are her numerous brushes and bombs.

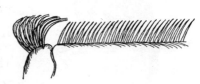

A Bee's Brush and Comb

33

HER WINGS

P OLLENLESS and honeyless Miss Apis leaves home. She returns with her sac full of honey and her baskets full of pollen.

That is, if she is fortunate she returns, for I regret to say that certain birds, being fond of honey, take it, bee and all.

They do not stop her and say, "Your honey or your life!" but swallow her whole and talk about it afterwards; that is, if they talk about it at all.

Down their throat she goes, honey-sac and long brown tongue, twelve thousand six hundred and three eyes and curious legs, all at once. Not so much as an eyes escapes, so far as I have ever heard.

Bee eating

Then these birds sit on a branch and "look as innercent as yer mammy's mockin' bird," as Uncle Remus would say, just

34

as if they had never eaten a bee in their lives, nor even thought of such a thing. But if she is fortunate she gets home.

She does not walk home, nor yet run; she flies.

For, as you know, she has wings. Dainty wings they are too. They are transparent and colorless like glass, and are very thin and delicate. They shine in the light, or you would scarcely notice them.

Miss Apis seems to have only two wings, though really there are four of them.

Whatever Miss Apis has she appears always to have in abundance; and when wings are in question, she must needs have four, although birds and dragons and such economical creatures are content with two.

She can fold her four wings down very neatly over her back when she wants to walk about, but when she starts to fly, she spreads them out, a pair on each side of her body.

 If the two wings on either side were to separate from each other and let the air between them her flight  would be spoiled, and she would go tumbling along in an ungainly and mortifying manner.

That this may not happen, she hooks the upper large wing and the lower small one together, when she raises them for flight, so that the two are as firm as though they were but one. She is enabled to do this by a row of hooks on the lower wing which fit into a groove on the upper wings, as you can see in the picture. The wings fit so closely together when hooked that you would not discover there were two, unless you looked very carefully indeed.

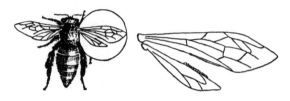

With her wings safely locked together, away she goes, sure and swift.

When she closes them, the smaller ones slip under the larger ones out of the way.

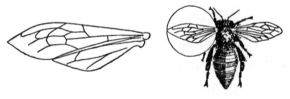

You see, four wings are handy when one wants to close them and have them out of the way, but two are best to fly with.

So, being a somewhat eccentric and withal ingenious individual, as you may have observed for yourself before this, Miss Apis has two wings to fly with, but four to fold away.

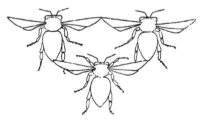

HOW SHE HEARS
AND SMELLS

M ISS APIS can hear and she can smell, though just how she hears, since she has no ears, and just how she smells, since she has no nose, puzzled people for a long time.

The truth is , she is able to do these things because of her antennæ, which you remember, are the two feelers that stand out from her face. These antennæ or feelers, are jointed, having one long joint next to the face, and a number of short joints forming a very movable tip. The long joint serves 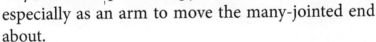 especially as an arm to move the many-jointed end about.

If Miss Apis's eyes seem to us wonderful, what shall we think of her antennæ? For though she has no ears, she has thousands of what we might call "hearing-spots" on the short joints of her antennæ. She also has thousands of "smell-hollows" on these remarkable antennæ joints. The hearing-spots and smell-hollows are very, very small, so that we can see them only by means of the microscope.

End of Antenna showing hairs

The antennæ are also covered with short, sensitive hairs which make them very good feelers, able to tell Miss Apis what kind of substance she is touching. They thus serve for eyes in the dark hive. You would not think Miss Apis needed any more eyes, but one cannot expect absolute perfection in this world, even in eyes, or even in Miss Apis, and the truth is that Miss Apis's many eyes are probably unable to help her in the dark.

Some creatures, like cats, can see in the dark, but Miss Apis is obliged to rely upon her antennæ for information when she goes into a dark place.

So you see these antennæ are very important and valuable. But you have not yet heard all. When bees have anything to say to each other they say it by means of their antennæ. Just how this is done I cannot say, as I do not know. But they manage it somehow.

When two bees meet they cross antennæ in a friendly way, instead of shaking hands and asking after each

"How do you do?"

other's health; that is, if they are friends, they do. If they are not members of the same family, I am sorry to say they fight. Two sisters, however, never fight.

Miss Apis's very life depends upon her antennæ. By means of them she hears, smells, discovers the nature of objects about her, and communicates with her fellow-bees.

When she is awake her antennæ are almost always

in motion, and she is constantly touching the flowers with them, or examining everything with which she comes in contact.

If anything happens to them, if they get broken off, or badly injured, poor little Miss Apis behaves very much like a rudderless boat at sea. She does not seem to know how to get anywhere, but moves about in an aimless sort of way. She does not eat or do her work, and in a short time she dies.

Naturally these priceless helpers need to be well taken care of. Dust and pollen must not be allowed to clog up the hearing and smelling organs, nor interfere with the sensitive hairs.

Since you have found Miss Apis provided with so many toilet articles, you will not be surprised that she has combs and brushes on purpose to keep her antennæ clean.

Yes, she has a comb and a brush on each front leg for that very purpose. You can see these curious little "antennæ cleaners," as they are called, with the naked eye on the bumble-bee, and you can see them very well indeed with an ordinary magnifying glass. They are on the inside of the leg at X and A.

There is a circular opening at A just large enough for the antennæ to fit into. It is bordered by a sort of round comb that reminds us of those combs little girls sometimes wear.

Only this comb is very small and the teeth point outward.

At the end of the joint above, at X, a stiff flap hangs down.

When the leg is bent the flap is brought down in front of the circular opening, as you see in the picture. When Miss Apis wishes to clean her antenna, which is very often, she raises her leg above her head, and draws it down over her antenna, which slips into the circular opening. Then she bends her leg, the flap holds the antenna in place and she draws that precious organ through the cleaner. The teeth in the round comb on one side and the sharp edges of the flap or brush on the other clean off every particle of dust.

You can see her almost any time drawing first one antenna, then the other, through the useful and remarkable little cleaners provided for the purpose. She will often stop in the middle of her honey-gathering to do it, for she seems to feel uncomfortable if her antennæ are not as clean as clean can be.

Cleaning her antenna

The brush at S is used to clean out the round comb on the opposite leg.

As you can imagine, it was a long time before

people understood the uses of Miss Apis's antennæ; but about two hundred years ago Mr. Francis Huber, a Swiss gentleman who loved bees, found out a part of the secret. He discovered that the honey-bee smells and feels with her antennæ. All who love bees ought to know and love Huber, for he spent many, many years studying the bees and finding out wonderful things about them.

I think you will like to hear his story.

When only a boy he was very fond of nature, and very fond of study. He read so constantly that he ruined his eyes and when still a young man became blind. This did not stop his work, however, for he had two friends who were eyes for him. One was the young lady to whom he was engaged to be married. When he became blind, her friends tried to persuade her to leave him, but she would not.

She insisted upon marrying him and taking care of him. Huber and his wife lived in happiness for a great many years, and Huber said that he did not realize he was blind until his wife died.

Huber's other friend was a man named Francis Burnens. Huber would tell Burnens just how to perform an experiment and just what to look for, and Burnens would do exactly as he was told, and then tell Huber all about it. In this way, Burnens did the seeing and Huber the thinking. Burnens was very patient and careful, and once he spent eleven days, scarcely stopping to sleep, in examining every bee in two hives.

Think what a task that was! I believe he drenched

the bees with water so they would not sting, and then examined them one by one. It was owing to the careful work of Burnens that Huber was able to make a number of important discoveries about bees.

A good many of the interesting facts we know to-day about bees we owe to blind Huber. He invented a hive which opened like the leaves of a book, so that he could at any time see what was going on inside, or—rather Burnens could see and tell him.

People to-day sometimes use narrow hives with glass sides, so that everything the bees do can be watched. Some schools have such a hive fastened in a window; this is very interesting for the children.

Bees do not willingly work in a light place, and they do not seem to enjoy being watched, so often they

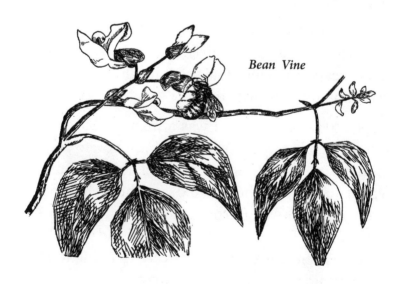

Bean Vine

smear the sides of the glass hive all over with bee glue, which prevent curious eyes from looking in.

Where bees are handled a good deal, they become quite tame. They seem to recognize their keeper. Bee-keepers very often have little machines by which they can puff smoke upon the bees. This does not hurt them, but makes them quiet, so the honey can be taken out and the bees handled.

HER STING

O THER things than birds sometimes catch Miss Apis, toads and frogs, for instance, and sometimes boys do it; but no boy catches her in his fingers without being punished for it. She has a dagger for such occasions, and it is not her tongue dagger either. It is as far from that as it can be, for it is at the extreme tip of her abdomen.

Of course, belonging to Miss Apis, it is a remarkable dagger. Sharp! My! If you do not believe me, just touch it.

Sharpness, however, is not unusual in daggers; all daggers are more or less sharp, though few as sharp as Miss Apis's.

But the thing that dis-

Be careful, Miss Apis!

tinguishes her dagger and makes it more terrible than any other, is its barbs. Generally daggers are smooth, and make a clean cut, coming out as easily as they go in. Not so Miss Apis's dagger. Although it is so tiny that we cannot see any barbs with the naked eye, still they are there. Instead of being smooth, it is fuller of barbs than a fish-hook, as you can see in the picture, which is a very much enlarged view of Miss Apis's sting. For while an ordinary fish-hook has but one or two barbs, this little stinger has *ten pairs!* It is not an easy matter to get a fish-hook out of your finger if it gets in beyond the barbs, as those of you who have ever had such an unpleasant experience know very well. If one pair of barbs hold so well, think how well *ten* pairs must hold! They hold altogether *too* well, as we shall see presently.

An ordinary fish-hook

Miss Apis's dagger magnified

Miss Apis's sting is not all in one piece, although it seems to be and it requires very careful examination to discover that it is made of three parts.

It is a sort of sheath with a groove running its whole length. Into this groove fit two lances that can move up and down in the groove. When Miss Apis decides to sting you, she first drives the sharp point of her sheath into you. This has a few barbs to keep it from slipping out again. Then one after the other the lances, each with its ten strong barbs, are thrust in. Deeper and deeper they are forced until they are as deep in as they can go. After all, the wound they make is very, very small, no worse that the prick of a fine needle, in fact. Then why does it hurt so? Ah, that is another question.

Miss Apis's barbed sting reminds us of the ugly weapons sometimes used by savages, and like the cruel savages, she too poisons her weapon.

That is why it hurts us so. A jet of poison is pumped down the hollow sting from a poison bag in her body, and is forced into the wound through an opening in the five lower barbs on each lance. So when Miss Apis stings us, we get ten jets of poison pumped into the little hole she makes in our skin.

Miss Apis's pleasant weapon is her constant companion, and she is very free to use it, excepting when the aforementioned birds snap her up so quickly, and swallow her down so fast, that she has not time to get over

Wild Blackberry

her surprise sufficiently to use her sting before she is a dead bee.

You may think she never stings when she is dead, but I have heard otherwise. However, that is another story. The birds that swallow her must sometimes get stung, but they do not seem to object; perhaps they enjoy it.

If you really want to know whether Miss Apis is willing to sting if she gets the chance, pick her up some day when she is getting nectar from a flower.

You will learn several things. First, that the best thing you can do under the circumstances is to let her go as soon as possible, and pursue some other path to knowledge.

But if you are a philosopher, you will not fail to observe what a very convenient position her sting occupies, as convenient for its purpose as the pollen-baskets are for theirs. She twists her jointed abdomen about so that you will have hard work to take hold of her where she cannot plunge her sting into you.

The entrance of this little sting gives rise to sensations out of all proportion to its size.

A sting so small that you can hardly see it produces a pain so large that you do not seem to have room for any other feeling. Presently the spot about the tiny hole made by the sting begins to swell until it may become several times as large as Miss Apis herself. That, you

know, is because she takes good care to pump poison into the wound.

This poison of hers is a reliable, warranted-never-to-fail irritant. If a whole hive of bees were to set upon you and sting you at once you might be made very sick by it, as well as have to suffer great torture.

It is said that people have even died from such mishaps.

We see that little Miss Pepper-pot is not so innocent as she looks flying about among the flowers.

Still, as I said, you cannot blame her for using her sting, and if she ever *does* use it on you, do not get angry, but pull it out, then put some mud on the place and try to remember that when it stops hurting, you will feel better.

Mud is a very good remedy, and, like Miss Apis's sting, is generally at hand.

There is another consolation about getting stung; if it happens often enough, the sting in time ceases to poison you!

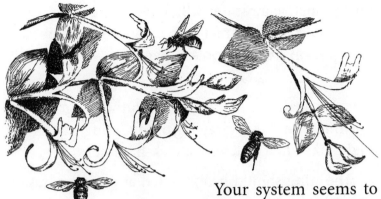

Your system seems to become used to the poison, so that it gradually loses its effect and its power to injure.

Still, I should not advise any one to try this remedy; it is too hard on the bees,—to say nothing of this unpleasant consequence to yourself.

For poor little Miss Apis, with her many eyes, her honey-sac, her complicated tongue and legs and all the rest, pays a terrible penalty for losing her temper and stinging people.

You remember her sting is barbed like a fish-hook; and if you have gone fishing much, you know how hard it is to pull a fish-hook out of anything into which it happens to get fastened.

Well, when Miss Apis recklessly plunges ten pairs of barbs into the tough skin of your finger, she cannot pull them out again; and in her efforts to do so, out comes sting, poison-bag and all, and off she goes, hurt much worse than you are, for she will surely die as a result of her loss.

She has left her poor savage little sting in your

finger, much against her will, however; and your first care should be to extract it so as not to press out any more poison from the poison bag.

This you can do by pressing the flat edge of a penknife against your skin close to the sting, but not touching it, and then drawing out the sting, just as you might take out a tack with a tack-hammer.

The sting should be extracted at once, because if it remains in your finger its muscles continue to work, even though the sting is now entirely separated from the bee, and every bit of poison will be pumped out of the poison bag into your finger.

So you see Miss Apis's sting continues to do the best it can, and to hurt you as much as possible, even after it has been completely torn from her body.

In fact, if you touch a sting newly removed from a bee, you will get stung by it. There is no doubt that it is a very reliable weapon.

In her fright and anger, Miss Apis does not stop to consider what will happen if she stings you, but stings first and thinks afterwards.

One should never sting first and think afterwards. One should always think first and not sting at all, unless it becomes absolutely necessary.

There *are* cases where one might better sting and die than live and not sting, but such cases are rare.

The American Revolution is one of them, but that happened a long time ago and has nothing to do with bees, anyway.

In spite of her reliable sting, Miss Apis is often eaten.

A good many birds are fond of bees, and other creatures, particularly bears, eat them.

It is truer to say that bears like *honey*, but they are willing to eat it, bees and all.

Bears are great honey eaters, and there are many stories told of their efforts to get honey. They will upset hives, and do not seem to mind being stung at all.

There is one story of a tame bear that used to take honey out of a bottle. He would lick out all he could reach, then turn the bottle up and let the honey run into his mouth. Usually it ran into his eyes as well, but that did not seem to trouble him.

A good many creatures are fond of bees and honey, so you see dangers beset Miss Apis's path, and even the pleasant occupation of gathering sweets from flowers is not without its drawbacks.

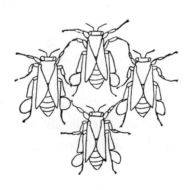

MISS APIS AND HER SISTERS

L ADEN with pollen and nectar, Miss Apis starts homeward.

People used to think she flew in a straight line to the hive, and so they called the shortest distance from one place to another a "bee line."

But she does not fly in a straight line,—far from it.

Whoever has "made a bee line for home"—that is a *true* bee line—must have followed a very indirect course indeed.

When Miss Apis has filled her honey-sac, and is ready to go home, she first mounts up into the air, not straight up, but round and round in a spiral, and when high enough she starts toward home—but not in a straight line. She makes a long curve to the right, and then to the left, to the right again, then to the left, and so on.

I do not know why she does this, but no doubt there is a good reason for it. Perhaps it makes it harder for bee-eating birds to catch her. It certainly is not easy to follow her flight with the eyes, until one has practiced enough to become accustomed to it.

When Miss Apis reaches home, she finds a large family.

There are her sisters, to begin with. She generally has many thousands of sisters just like herself, and they are all named Apis Mellifica.

This might be confusing if they called each other by name, that is, by the name we have given them. But of course, they do not do that.

I do not know what they call each other, but I do know that they are as much alike as one pea is like another. They all have twelve thousand six hundred small eyes and three large ones, a folding tongue, a honey-sac, wings that lock together, extraordinary legs, and several other useful and curious things.

Having watched Miss Apis going from flower to flower in the sunshine, you may think that this pleasant duty is all there is in her life. But oh, how mistaken you are!

Wait until you see her at home! There is as much work to be done in her house as in anybody's and she does it too. She works very hard, and , in fact, with her sisters, does *all* the work. Nobody else in the family does any, and so she is called the worker bee.

For you must know that she and her thousands of sisters, who are as like her as one pea is like another, are not the only members of the family.

THE BROTHERS

T HERE are the drones, their brothers. These fine
gentlemen never gather honey or pollen, nor do
any work in the hive.

In fact, they are scarcely able to feed themselves,
and very much like to have their sisters feed them.

They are handsome fellows, and somewhat larger
than their little worker sisters.

 They have large round heads, with
enormous compound eyes that meet
on top and crowd the other three eyes
down in front, between them. They
have more than twice as many facets
in their eyes as the workers. Their
antennæ are long and very sensitive. They have large
bodies covered with a coat of soft brown down, very
pretty to look at, and their wings are large.

That they are so helpless, I am glad to say, is not their
fault. Mr. Apis Mellifica has no honey-sac, so he could
hardly be expected to go out and try to bring home

honey. He could not get it even if he had a honey-sac in which to store it, because his tongue is so short and so weak. He can eat honey from the honey-comb in the hive, or from any easily obtained supply; but that is the best he can do.

So Mr. Drone Apis Mellifica leaves the sweet occupation of gathering nectar to his sister, Miss Worker Apis Mellifica.

As for pollen, the drone has no baskets in which to carry it, so there is an end to that.

And as for working in the hive, he is no better off for tools to work with than he is for a honey-sac, a serviceable tongue, and pollen baskets.

In fact, there is nothing for him to do but to stay at home and be taken care of like a gentleman of leisure.

This he does to perfection. He stands about with his hands in his pockets, so to speak, and lets his little brown sisters feed him, which they do by allowing him to put his tongue into their mouths. On warm,

His little brown sister feeds him

sunny days, he flies out to see the world and to try his fortune.

Occasionally a drone meets the young queen of another hive, also out to see the world. When this happens they mate, but she stays with him only a short time, and then goes back to her own hive and leaves him.

The poor fellow has no sting at all, so he cannot

defend himself, or avenge an insult. We may pick him up, if we can catch him, with no fear of being stung, and may say anything to him or about him that we please.

Basketless, stingless, with no honey-sac, and no serviceable nectar-gathering tongue, he is almost as helpless as a Chinese lady.

Only she is purposely made helpless, and he is born so.

A Chinese girl baby has as good feet as any baby, and they would grow as large as other people's if it were not the fashion for the mothers to squeeze the poor little tootsie-wootsies into small ugly shoes that hurt the babies terribly and make them as cross as crabs. It serves their mothers right, too, when they are cross. Think of crippling them all their lives so they can neither work nor do anything useful.

In China the people consider it a disgrace to work, and the rich people cripple their girl babies to show that it is not necessary for them to work.

It is not considered a disgrace to work in the hive, however, nor in any other really civilized community.

In fact, all the bees in the hive work very hard, excepting the drones, and they generally form a very small proportion of the whole number.

The drone is an idler because he is so made that it is impossible for him to work.

But he is happy, and flies about in the sun taking whatever good comes to him without finding fault.

His sisters are glad to work for him, and he is glad to have them do so.

THE QUEEN

O NE would expect to find a mother in so large and
flourishing a family, and you will not be surprised
to hear that there is one.

Queen Apis Mellifica is the mother of the hive, and
is by far the most important member of the community,
as I suppose a queen always is—or should be, if she is
a true queen.

Queen Apis is a true queen, as she shows by working
harder than any other bee in the hive. Of course her
work is different from that of the workers, else why
should she be a queen? She does not carry nectar and
pollen, and make honey-comb, and care for the young
bees, but she does something just as difficult and just
as important.

Like the drone, she has no honey-sac and no pollen
baskets, though both queen and drone have plenty of
brushes on their legs to keep themselves clean. Her
wings are small, and she has a very short tongue. Her
head is small in proportion to her body, as are also her

eyes, which have fewer facets than the workers' eyes, and she has short antennæ.

In this picture of the heads of the queen, the drone, and the worker, you can readily tell which is which.

You see the queen expects to be taken care of all her days, and so does not need to be as well provided with sense organs as the workers.

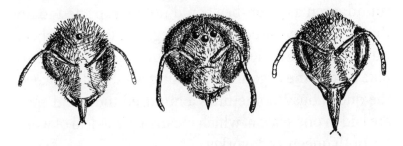

Like the workers, and unlike the drones, she has a sting, but she very seldom uses it. In fact, you can handle her with as little fear of being stung as you can handle a drone.

The queen's sting is very, very precious, and she will not run the risk of losing it by stinging you.

There is only one queen in a hive, and she very seldom flies abroad. There is too much to be done at home, for we must not forget that she is really the *mother* of the whole colony. The workers are her daughters, and the drones her sons. We call her a queen, but she is queen only in the sense that every true mother is a queen in her home.

If the people who named her long ago had known as much about bees as we know today, they doubtless would have called her the mother-bee instead of the queen-bee.

The chief occupation of the queen-bee is to lay eggs. She lays the eggs for the whole colony.

Sometimes she lays as many as three thousand in one day.

She does not keep this up day after day the year round; even a queen-bee could not be expected to do that. But to lay three thousand eggs a day for a short time will furnish plenty of work for those who have to take care of the eggs and the young bees, and will keep the queen busy. Sometimes a hundred thousand eggs are laid in one season, which means a great deal of work for both queen and workers.

The ancients believed that bees gathered their young off the leaves of trees, or from the flowers of honeywort, the reed, or the olive. There was another superstition, that bees came forth from the decayed bodies of animals, and Virgil, who wrote much better Latin than most people can write English, soberly gives us a recipe for producing bees from the dead bodies of cattle!

Virgil's power to write well was greater than his knowledge of Natural History, which is not surprising, since there were no microscopes in those days.

To-day we know that if there are to be young bees, eggs must first be laid.

Bees cannot be picked from trees or flowers, or any other object, and carried home.

The queen-bee has to lay an egg for every one of the many bees that fill a hive.

And now you can understand why Queen Apis is so exceedingly particular about using her sting; for her sting is her ovipositor as well.

Ovipositor means egg-placer, for *ovi* comes from a Latin word, meaning egg, and *positor* from another Latin word, meaning "to place." It is with this that she places the eggs just where she wants them to be.

The ovipositor is made very much like the sting of the worker; and as the eggs ripen they pass through the long tube of the ovipositor, which guides them to the right place in the comb.

If the queen were to lose her sting, she would no longer be able to lay the eggs, and so the colony would soon die out.

For worker-bees live only a few months at the best, and sometimes only a few weeks, so the queen, who lives four or five years, and sometimes even longer, has to keep on laying eggs in order to keep her large household supplied with new members as the old die off.

It is no wonder, therefore, that she will not sting.

The queen takes no care of the eggs, nor of the young bees. She leaves all that to her daughters, the workers. She does not even feed herself much of the time.

But the workers are glad to take care of her. They prepare a special food for her, better than the food the other grown-up bees get, which is quite proper, as such a bee could not be expected to eat ordinary food.

Queen Apis has tasters, as did the old kings of France and England. Only the king's taster ate a little of the king's dish in his Majesty's presence, that he might be sure nobody had poisoned it, for they were fond of poisoning kings in those days.

But Queen Apis is not afraid of poison. She knows her children love her too well for that, and that they taste her food out of love to her. In fact, they do more than taste it, they swallow and digest the bee-bread and honey, and in their bodies it is made into a very nutritious food with which they feed their queen.

When she is hungry she goes to a worker bee, inserts her short tongue into its mouth, and takes what she wants, though sometimes she eats honey from the combs as well.

Occasionally bees feed one another on honey in this way, and they also feed the drones.

If you put a bee just caught and with her sac full of honey on a window-pane with a bee from the same hive that has had nothing to eat for an hour or two, you will see a pretty sight. The hungry bee will go to her newly arrived companion, and as soon as they have crossed antennæ and discovered they are friends, the hungry sister will present her tongue. Then the other will open her jaws and doubtless proceed to force up the honey from the honey-sac to her mouth for the benefit of her hungry sister.

The one that takes the sweets usually raises her wings slightly as though expressing her pleasure and satisfaction at thus unexpectedly obtaining a meal.

There is good reason for feeding the queen with "royal jelly," as her food is called.

The formation of eggs uses up a good deal of food material as well as a good deal of strength.

If Queen Apis's strength were used up in digesting food, for it takes a good deal of strength to digest food properly, how do you suppose she could lay all those eggs?

She could not possibly do it. The workers seem to know this, and so they save her strength in every possible way.

They give her an abundance of the best of food, and they do all the work, not even asking her to take any care of the little bee-babies when they are hatched.

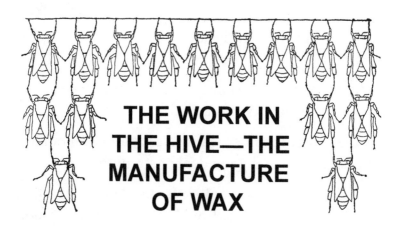

THE WORK IN THE HIVE—THE MANUFACTURE OF WAX

SINCE honey bees eat almost nothing but pollen and honey, a good store of these has to be laid up for winter use, as well as to feed all the young bees and the drones.

Gathering honey and pollen, however, is but a small part of our little worker's business.

If I tell you there is something very wonderful about Miss Apis that you have not yet heard, you will not be surprised.

Probably by this time you would be more surprised if you failed to hear something wonderful about her.

This that I am about to tell is quite as wonderful as her eyes, or her honey-sac, or her wings, or anything else.

She has pockets!

You do not think pockets are so very wonderful?

Well, neither do I, just ordinary commonplace, every-day pockets for carrying pencils and such things; but what about *wax* pockets? Not pockets made of wax, you understand, but pockets filled with wax.

Miss Apis has a head.

That is no news, I am aware, as most creatures have heads. But connected with her head by a short neck, as you know, she has a chest, which if you want to be scientific you must call a thorax. To this her legs and wings are fastened, and behind her thorax, and attached to it by a very slender waist, is the rest of her body, or as we must call it, her abdomen.

This abdomen is jointed; it is made of rings connected to each other by a skin-like membrane, and the rings fit close together under each other, or are drawn apart from each other to lengthen her abdomen.

There are six of these rings, and underneath four of them, on the under-side of her abdomen, are shallow hollows, two on each ring, and these eight hollows are the wax pockets.

The queen and the drones have no wax pockets; only the workers have them.

Miss Apis's Wax Pockets with the white wax showing in them

If you think Miss Apis gathers the wax somewhere and puts it into these pockets, you are as much mistaken as if you thought two and two were nine. She does not gather it; she *makes* it.

By this time you will understand she is rather peculiar.

When you undertake to store up honey, you must have something to put it in. You cannot put it on the floor or in a corner where everybody that went near it would stick fast, and where it would run out and be wasted.

You must have bottles, or cans, or jars, or something of that kind to put it in.

If you are a bee you cannot go to the store and buy these things; you have to make them. You have no glass to make them of, and would not know how if you had. So you gorge yourself with honey, eat all you possibly can, then go hang yourself up in the top of the hive and wait.

That is what the bees at the head of this chapter are doing.

And now you see how very important their hook-like toes are, for all they have to do is to turn up their toes and hook them fast to the hive or to the foot of another bee.

This time, you understand, the honey has actually been *eaten*, not stored away to be drawn back into the mouth again and deposited in the hive. It has been eaten, and the bee now keeps still while this heavy meal digests.

You and I, who have studied Physiology a little,

know that when people are able to digest much sugar they become fat. The sugar is someway turned into fat.

Eating a great deal of sugar is not the same thing as digesting a great deal, please remember that. When people eat a great deal of sugar, as, for instance, candy and other sweetmeats, at all hours of the day, it generally does not digest; it does something very different, and ultimately makes them sick. But bees are so happily constituted that they can digest all they eat.

When a bee eats so much honey that she can do nothing but sleep, as it were, until she gets over the effects, we might be tempted to call her a glutton. But we must not judge bees by ourselves. In some respects they are wiser than we. When a bee gorges herself with honey, she knows what she is doing. She knows she will not suffer from indigestion, for one thing, and she knows she will not become fat and clumsy for another. Of course the sweet meal must be disposed of in some way; and, in fact, there is formed from it a substance something like fat, only different.

This substance is wax, and it finds its way in liquid form through pores in the bee's body into the eight depressions on the under-side of the abdomen, where it hardens. We might say she *sweats* out the wax into her pockets.

When Miss Apis wants wax, then, she eats a hearty meal of honey and suspends herself in the hive for a nap while it digests. When she wakes up, her eight pockets are full of wax. It was Huber who first told us that wax is made from honey eaten by the bees.

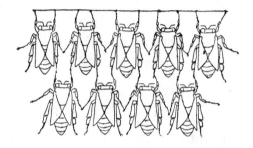

HONEY-COMB

W AX makes first-rate jars for storing honey. It is tight and firm, and prevents air and water from getting in. It is strong enough not to be injured by the weight of the bees walking over it.

You may be sure Miss Apis knows all this.

She is not surprised to find her pockets full of wax, and she knows just what to do with it.

Her hind legs are each provided with a pair of nippers for pulling the wax scales out of the pockets. You can best see them by looking at the inside of the leg. At the end of joint 4 at A are strong teeth that shut down on the hard plate at X on joint 5.

When she has pulled out the scales, she moistens them in her mouth with saliva, for they are too brittle at first to be useful. When they are thoroughly moistened and softened, she pulls them out into white bands.

Now she is all ready to make honey-cups.

First, in company with a number of her sisters, she sticks a little wax along one side of the hive near the top, then the six-sided cups or cells are begun.

This sounds easy enough, but suppose you try to make a six-sided cell of moist bees' wax and see how you succeed!

Of course you have not the best tools in the world for such work, for good as fingers may be for cutting with a scissors, or driving nails, or picking up pins, they would be poor tools for making cells of bees' wax.

Miss Apis is supplied with something better. You know about that. Those claws on her feet are admirable wax tools, and so are her jaws, and even her tongue, which she uses in the finer work of the cell.

The bees begin at the roof and build the comb downward.

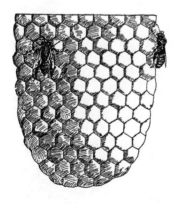

It is wonderful to think of the fairy structure growing there in the dark hive under the efforts of the industrious little bees.

They make six-sided cells lying close together, so as not to waste either room or wax.

No other shape would so well fill the space.

They have found this out; and as they want to put as many cells into as small a space as possible, the wise workers pat, and pull, and press the wax into hexagonal cups or jars.

Although many bees work together, and in the dark too, they keep watch over each other's movements in some way, and build the cells in rows, one row below the other, until they have a wall or sheet of cells reaching nearly to the bottom of the hive.

This sheet of cells we call a comb.

If you expect to find all the cells in a comb of exactly the same size and shape, you will be disappointed.

Miss Apis fills the space at her disposal with wonderfully regular six-sided cells, far better ones than you or I could make; but the rows are not always *perfectly* straight, and the cells are not always *perfectly* uniform in size, as they would be if made by machinery.

Miss Apis is not a machine, and for my part I like her work better than if it were perfectly regular.

As the comb hangs in the hive, the cells of course do not stand up with their open mouths at the top as we set a cup on the table, but they lie on their sides, which seems rather odd when we come to think of it.

Suppose you were to lay your fruit jars on their sides on the table in a row, and then pile another row above them, and so on.

You would have them nicely packed away, but how *could* you fill them without having the contents run out as fast as put in?

Miss Apis is able to overcome even that difficulty. She builds a double row of cells placed back to back, and opening of course in opposite directions.

The cells are not quite parallel with the floor of 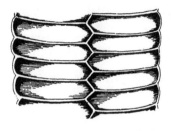 the hive, but their mouths are tipped up just a little, and they are slightly curved, as if Miss Apis were afraid the honey might run out if she laid them down too flat.

If you look into an empty cell of honey-comb, you will see that the cells in a sheet of comb are not exactly opposite to each other, but that the bottom of a cell on the right side of the comb overlaps the edges of three or four cells on the left side. That is, the cells are placed so that the bottom of one rests where three others on the opposite side come together, and sometimes overlaps a fourth.

You can easily see the edges of the opposite cells through the wax that forms the bottom of a cell, and you can understand that placing the cells this way makes the comb much stronger.

Now the comb is made and ready to be filled with honey.

Probably young bees that have not yet gone out of the hive in search of nectar, build the cells.

The rovers bring in nectar, and standing over the cells press it up from their honey-sacs. A great many loads are necessary to fill one cell, as each bee carries less than a drop at a time.

All day long in and out fly the bees, each one leaving her little load of honey to help to fill the honey-comb cells.

But why does not the honey run out as fast as it is put in? That question has not yet been answered.

It is easier to ask than to answer, unless you know more about natural philosophy than I think you do.

To begin with, honey is sticky. You know that as well as I do. And it will stick to honey cups as well as to anything else. When the bee puts a little drop in the bottom of a cup it tends to stick fast. A cellful of honey, however, is not sticky enough to keep from running out, as we know when we take off the cover to a honey-comb cell. To help the honey to stay in, the cells, as we know, are tilted up a little. The cells are small, and the liquid honey tends to remain in a small cell, just on that account,—which is a matter for Physics to explain. Then, when Miss Apis has her cell nearly full, she begins to put a cover over it. She begins at the bottom of the cell to put on this "cap," as it is called, and by the time she has finished the cap, the cell is as full of honey as she can get it, but there is a little air left in, which acts as a cushion, and keeps the honey from running against the cap.

So there is her honey-cup, filled and sealed.

Miss Apis fills her honey cell rather slowly, and leaves it uncapped for a few days until the extra water evaporates and the honey is "ripened."

You know very well that if you have molasses in an open dish, it becomes thicker as time goes on; that is because it loses its water by evaporation, and that is exactly what happens when honey is left uncapped for a while. It gets thicker and keeps better.

Miss Apis does not fill *all* of her fine little wax preserve jars with honey. If she did, what would become of the bee-bread?

We do not often see bee-bread in these days, because we have given Miss Apis little wooden frames for her honey-comb, and when we take these from the hive, only those containing pure honey are sent to market. If there is bee-bread in any of the frames, they are returned to the hive.

When Miss Apis comes home with her pollen baskets full, she scrapes out her load into a wax jar, or cell, as I suppose we ought to call it.

You remember the little crowbar she has on her middle leg for prying the sticky mass out of her pollen basket.

When the pollen, or bee-bread, as it

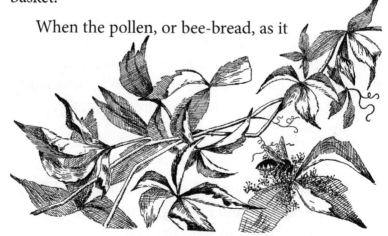

generally is called after Miss Apis has gathered it and mixed it with honey, has been pushed into the cell, it is patted down and perhaps a little more honey added to it. When the cell is full, it is capped over like the cells that contain honey.

Sometimes a whole comb will be filled with bee-bread, and sometimes a comb will contain part bee-bread and part honey.

Miss Apis is fond of bee-bread, but we are not. We gladly take away her honey, but we do not care to rob her of her bee-bread. It has a curious taste which I should like to describe to you, but I can only say it tastes like bee-bread, and like nothing else in the world that I know of.

Miss Apis has a habit of storing the honey in the top of the hive, and that is where, in our new-fashioned hives, we put the little wooden frames we want her to fill. When she has filled them, all we have to do is to open the top of the hive and lift them out; that is, unless she has glued them fast.

Woodbine

Miss Apis is very particular about having everything firm and tight in her hive. She does not want honey-combs tumbling about her ears, breaking and spilling what is in them, so whenever there is half an excuse to do so she glues them fast. She stops up all the holes in her hive, too, with glue; that is, if there are any holes.

No doubt this glue is very useful when she builds in hollow trees, or when her hive is old and rickety.

But people generally take care of the hives, and build them tight or else stop up the holes.

Miss Apis's glue is a perfect nuisance to the bee-keeper. She seems to think she must daub everything over with it, whether necessary or not, and she fastens the frames so tightly, if the bee-keeper is not on the watch, that it is hard work to get them out of the hive.

The only way is to watch and take out the frames before she has time to glue them fast.

You wonder where she gets her glue? Why, she just finds it. She sometimes scrapes it off from the sticky buds of the poplar or cherry tree, or from other plants. Huber watched his bees scrape bee-glue from wild poplar buds. Miss Apis brings the glue home in her pollen baskets. It is brown and shiny like resin, and spoils the looks of whatever it touches. But Miss Apis does not seem to care much for mere looks.

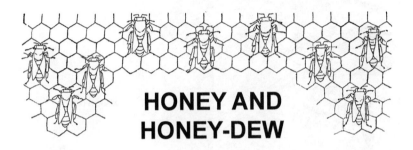

HONEY AND
HONEY-DEW

M ISS Apis is probably as proud of her hive when she gets it stored full of honey and bee-bread, as your mother is of her pantry when she gets the jelly and preserves done in the fall.

At least, I should think she would be.

It is a very cunning art to take nectar from the flowers, and in one's honey-sac change it into delicious honey.

It is not every creature that can do that. In fact, I know of but one or two besides Miss Apis and her near relatives that can.

Although the nectar is changed to honey, it still retains its own flavor, so that the bee-keepers can often tell by the taste what kind of flowers honey is made from.

Miss Apis is very particular about the quality of her honey, and does not like to mix up different kinds. If she starts out to gather white clover honey, she will

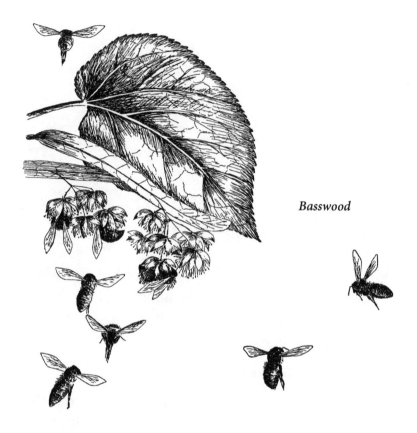

Basswood

visit the clover fields all day, and for many days, and pass by other flowers, rather than mix their nectar with the clover nectar.

White clover honey is delicate and delicious, and bees are very fond of visiting the white clover heads. Honey-bees do not gather much honey from the red clover, because the little flower tubes are too long for their tongues, and generally they cannot reach the nectar.

Bumble-bees love the red clover, but you shall hear a story about that later.

Sweet clover yields good honey, and where it grows the bees gather a great deal from it.

The fragrant flowers of the basswood are great favorites with the bees, and when a basswood tree is in bloom, it sometimes sounds like an enormous bee-hive, there are so many bees after its honey.

Most people who live in the north are familiar with the dark-colored buckwheat honey, and those who live far south know the clear delicate orange-blossom honey.

Sometimes bees gather honey from poisonous plants, but that does not happen very often in this country. When you read Xenophon's "Anabasis," you will learn how Xenophon's whole army were poisoned by eating some honey they found while marching through Asia. The Retreat of the Ten Thousand is a very interesting story, and I hope you will hurry and get old enough to read the "Anabasis."

Miss Apis sometimes gathers other sweets than flower-juice. I am sorry to say she will even steal the honey from other bees if she can get it.

Sometimes she takes cider, but that makes very poor honey indeed. When ripe fruits split open, or the wasps bite holes in them, Miss Apis may sometimes be seen taking her share of the fruit juice.

It is not often, however, that Miss Apis preserves fruit juice; she leaves that for us to do.

She does collect honey-dew, though, and sometimes will fill her hive full of honey made from it.

Probably you do not know what honey-dew is; it is not everybody that does know, but I do, and I am going to tell.

You all have heard of the aphides, the ants' cows?

You know they are tiny little insects with two horns on their backs. They give out a sweet liquid of which the ants are very fond. We are told that some ants take care of the aphides, protect them and treat them as if they were indeed little insect cows.

At certain seasons of the year the aphides are very

abundant. We sometimes call them plant-lice, and I am sure you have all seen them on rose bushes, and lilies, and other garden plants. Sometimes they are green, sometimes brown, sometimes they have wings, sometimes not. They are very curious little creatures, and sometime you must learn more about them.

Aphides enlarged

An aphis puts her bill into the skin of a leaf, and there she stays and sucks out its juice, which you can imagine is not very good for the leaf.

Some of the juice which the aphides eat is changed into the sweet liquid the ants are so fond of; and if there are no ants to eat it, the aphides are obliged to get rid of it, and they squirt it out in the air.

I have stood under a tulip-tree and watched a perfect shower of this honey-dew come raining down from the countless aphides on the leaves. The aphides stay on the under-side of the leaves and the honey-dew falls on the upper side of the leaves below them. Sometimes the leaves of a tree or a bush will shine as if they had been varnished, because of the honey-dew that covers them. Such leaves are sticky to the touch, too, and, in fact, become very disagreeable, as dust settles on the sticky surface.

I once saw all the plants in the Carolina Mountains covered with this honey-dew. The season had been dry, which is what the aphides like, and they were over everything.

The little mountain children used to pick these sweet leaves and lick off the honey-dew. You see, they have no candy in the mountains, and the children took the honey-dew without waiting for the bees to make it into honey.

But bees and children are not the only lovers of honey-dew.

I have often watched the squirrels lick it from the leaves.

They take a leaf between their paws and hold it to their mouths, while their little tongues lick the leaf all over. It is great fun to watch the squirrels do this, and I hope you will see it yourself some day. I do not know whether squirrels like candy, but I am perfectly sure they like honey-dew.

Honey-dew used to be a great mystery to people, and very funny notions were held regarding it.

Pliny, an old Latin naturalist, supposed it was "the perspiration of the sky, the saliva of the stars, or the moisture deposited by the atmosphere while purging itself, corrupted by its admixture with the mists of earth."

We know that it is not the perspiration of the sky, nor the saliva of the stars, but just the work of the little aphides.

There are many people still living who think the honey-dew goes up as a sort of mist from the earth, and falls again as a sweet dew on the leaves.

Bees like the honey-dew very much, and I have eaten honey made from it, but I must confess I did not like it.

Some honey-dew is said to make very good honey, but I prefer to have the bees bring my honey from the flowers.

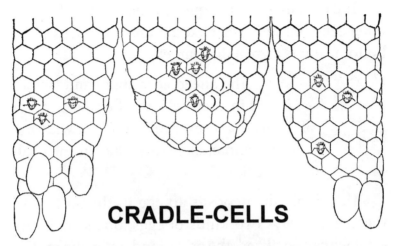

CRADLE-CELLS

SOME of Miss Apis's wax cells serve the purpose of preserve-jars, as we have seen. Indeed, they all do, when we come to think of it.

They do not all preserve honey and bee-bread, however.

You have not forgotten that the queen-bee sometimes lays as many as three thousand eggs a day. Well, each little egg must have a cell of comb all to itself.

You can imagine that the wax-makers and cell-builders do not have a chance to grow lazy in the busy season of egg-laying; for if the queen does not lay three thousand eggs every day, she may upon some days, and she always lays at least enough to satisfy any reasonable lover of hard work.

The cradle-cells of the drones are the same as the honey-cells, but the worker cells are about one-fifth smaller.

You see, the workers are smaller than the drones, and so can lie in smaller cradles.

The cradle-cell of the queen is not shaped like the other cells, but somewhat like a thimble. It opens at the bottom, and is a great deal larger.

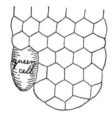
The queen goes about and lays an egg in each cell. She first puts in her head and examines the cell with her antennæ, as if to make sure it is all right.

This done, she deposits an egg in the bottom of the cell. She lays two kinds of eggs, one kind being what we call fertilized, the other kind unfertilized. The fertilized eggs always hatch into workers or queens, the unfertilized always hatch into drones. The queen is able to fertilize the eggs, or not, as she pleases.

As soon as an egg is laid, the queen pays no further attention to it. It is now the turn of the nurse-bees. The nurse-bees are the younger ones that have not yet gone out of the hive.

For about three days after the egg is laid, you could see no change in it.

Perhaps you think it needs no attention, but a hen would not think so. *She* knows that eggs have to be kept warm in order to hatch, and so she sits on her own eggs with her feathers tucked down warm all about them. Miss Apis, too, understands that eggs need to be kept warm. She has no feathers, but she has a warm little fuzzy body, and when the eggs are laid, she and her sisters cluster over the comb to keep them warm.

The ancients held a good many wrong ideas, and a

good many right ones, about bees, and our Latin friend Pliny was not altogether wrong when he said bees sat upon their eggs like hens.

In about three days the eggs hatch, but not into pretty downy bees with gauzy wings. No, indeed! If you were to see what hatches out of a bee's egg you would not imagine that queer thing could ever make a bee. It is a little white atom, with no legs 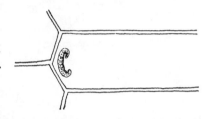 and no wings, and looks like a maggot. Here is a picture of one very much enlarged. It may not look like a bee, but still it is a baby bee.

If you do not like to call it a bee, you may call it a *larva*. For *larva* is the name we give to the first form of an insect after it leaves the egg.

This little larva is born hungry, and the kind nurse-bees, knowing that, feed it with plenty of—what shall I call it? Bee-milk, perhaps. This bee-milk is manufactured by the nurses in glands in their heads; it is very nutritious, and is the same as the royal jelly with which the queen is fed. They place the food in the cell with the larva, and watch to see that it always has enough. They feed it with honey and pollen as it grows older; and how it does eat!

In a few days it has grown so large that it almost fills its cradle-cell.

It would not do to let this ravenous infant grow entirely out of bounds, but I doubt if you could guess what the nurse-bees do to prevent it. They simply stop feeding it.

That is certainly a sure way to check its growth; only 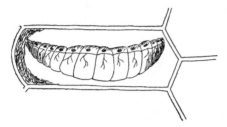 most babies, if treated so, would make up their minds that life without dinner was not worth living, and would die right off.

But bee-babies do not die; they wait to see what will happen next. It would take a long time for anybody but a bee to guess what happens next.

It is rather a peculiar performance, but Miss Apis's performances are usually peculiar.

She caps over the cell of the baby-bee.

It would be difficult to imagine an easier way of disposing of a baby,—bottle it up like a jar of pickles or a cell of honey.

It is not much trouble to take care of *such* babies.

They only need to be kept warm. Meantime, the infant thus disposed of spins for itself a soft little silken night-cap.

You see, it has nothing else to do. It cannot get anything to eat, and they do not give it so much as a rubber ring to bite on, as far as I know; so it amuses itself spinning a night-cap, or a soft little cocoon, about the upper part of its fat little bottled-up body.

Some babies might cry under the circumstances;

but I doubt if this baby could do that even if it wanted to, for how *could* it cry with its mouth full of silk?

The silk for its cocoon comes out of its mouth, strange to say,—or rather out of a little hole in its lip,—and I have no doubt it is great fun for it to draw out the fine thread and spin.

Then it changes shape. You see, it is really an infant Miss Apis, so we cannot be surprised that it should perform in queer ways, even at that tender age.

It changes from a larva into a pupa.

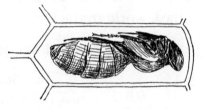

If you do not know what a pupa is, it is time you did.

It is the same as a chrysalis. If you do not know what a chrysalis is, look at the picture and you will see one in the cell.

You see, it is not a larva, nor yet a perfect insect, but something halfway between the two.

When Baby Apis becomes a pupa, she does nothing more wonderful than butterflies and many other insects do,—for they too become pupæ on the way to being grown up, just as we become boys or girls on the way to being men or women.

You may like to know that larva is a Latin word, and means *ghost*, or *mask*, for the larva is, in one sense, the ghost or mask of the perfect insect.

But what do you think pupa means?

It, too, is a Latin word, and means *doll*.

The pupa of insects is generally inactive, and does not seem to be alive, though, of course, it is alive, and so it is called a doll, or image of the insect.

Baby Apis remains a pupa for several days, then she makes up her mind that if they want to keep other babies in bottles, they may, but as for her, she has had enough of it, so she puts up her mouth and gnaws a hole the shape of a crescent in the cap they put over her, and probably peeps out to see the world,—rather a dark world in the hive, one would think.

Then she puts out her head.

Then out she comes, a lovely young bee, light-colored and downy, and with beautiful gauzy wings.

The cap that is put over the young bee is very porous, so the air can get in. Baby Apis may be bottled up with safety, but she must not be deprived of air, for if she is she will die.

The queen-bee is hatched from an egg exactly like that of the worker-bees. But this egg, as we know, lies in a large cell, and when it hatches, the nurse-bees fairly stuff the queen larva with food.

The worker infants get very little bee-milk; they have to eat honey and bee-bread, but the queen infant is fed almost entirely upon this precious food, this "royal jelly."

It is because she eats so much of this that she develops into a queen. Sometimes the queen in a hive dies or gets lost. Then what do you suppose the workers do? Why, go to work and make a new queen, of course.

It is a terrible thing for a hive to be without a queen, and the bees are very unhappy when it happens. But if they have eggs or very young larvæ they need not despair.

They enlarge a worker cell in which lies an egg or a very young larva, by tearing down the cells next to it. Then they feed the infant thus promoted to royalty upon queen's food, and, lo! the little creature becomes a queen.

Drones get much more royal jelly than workers, but no amount of feeding or starving will make them anything but drones.

It takes all the eggs three days to hatch, but the queen larva attains its growth in five and a half days, while it takes the worker six, and the drone, six and a half.

The queen spins her cocoon, changes into a pupa, and comes forth a perfect bee all in seven and a half days, while it takes the worker twelve days and the drone fourteen and a half to complete these changes.

If you do a little sum in addition, you will find that it takes sixteen days for an egg to become a queen-bee, twenty-one days for it to become a worker, and twenty-four days for a drone egg to become a drone.

As soon as the worker-bees hatch out, they go to work.

You already know what they do. They take care of the

queen, following her about and feeding her with royal jelly whenever she is hungry, which is very often.

They seem to be very fond of their hive-mother; and you will always see a little cluster of bees about her, caressing her with their antennæ, and paying her the greatest respect.

The workers also take care of the eggs and the young bees, but do not generally lay any eggs themselves; only the queen does that.

They make wax, build comb, and keep the hive clean, carrying out dead bees, or anything that does not belong in it.

No doubt they watch at the door, too. For bees keep sentinels always on guard to see that thieves and robbers do not come in and steal their honey.

If you knock on a hive, the sentinels will fly out to see what is the matter.

In a few days the young bees leave the home work to the newly hatched, and go forth to gather honey, and pollen, and bee-glue.

You ought to know that bee-glue is called *propolis*,—a word that means "before the city,"—and it is so named, because the bees use it to build fortifications in time of war.

Certain moths attack bee-hives by crawling in and laying their eggs in the corners. When the eggs hatch, the little caterpillar-like larvæ that come out of them eat the comb and spoil the honey. To keep them out, the bees sometimes build walls of propolis just inside the hive

Locust

door, making the entrance so narrow that only one bee can pass at a time. In this way the sentinels are better able to keep out the intruders.

Bees have been known to use propolis in strange ways. You know they chink up all the holes with it and glue the frames fast. Once, so the story goes, they glued a snail to the bottom of the hive. His snailship had crawled into the hive and the bees fastened his shell tightly to the floor. So, for going where he was not wanted, he found his house converted into a sepulchre.

Another story is of a mouse that went into a bee-hive. The bees stung him to death, but he was so large they could not remove him, so what did they do but cover him all over with propolis. Safe under the resinous bee-glue, his body could do no harm.

Bees breathe as well as other creatures; they take in pure air and give out impure. They do not do this by means of lungs, as we do, but through little holes in their sides. They cannot live without fresh air, and you can well imagine that a house as crowded as theirs needs careful ventilation.

They cannot lower the windows, because they have none, and they would not dare open any if they had them, for all sorts of creatures would come flying, and creeping, and running, and stealing in to get their precious honey.

The only openings to the hives, as we know, are the little holes at the bottom where the bees go in and out. How, then, do they get fresh air?

You will not be surprised to learn that Miss Apis has solved this problem in a very ingenious manner.

The only possible way of ventilating a hive through the little holes at the bottom is by fanning or pumping the air in and out.

The bees fan a current of air through the hive, by standing near the entrance holes and buzzing with their wings.

The buzzing sound is made by the rapid motion of the wings, and even one bee can cause quite a little breeze. When a number of them stand together just inside, and sometimes also just outside the hive, and fan, they produce currents of air strong enough to keep the crowded hive perfectly ventilated.

Bees are more careful to have plenty of fresh air than are people. Huber discovered that the air in the hive is nearly as pure as the air out of doors, and we should have reason to feel proud if our public buildings were as well ventilated as are the bee-hives.

THE FAMILY EXODUS

ONE cannot go on adding several thousand members a week to one's family without sooner or later being obliged to enlarge the house—or move out. The Apis people move out.

As soon as a young queen comes out of her cell, the old queen packs up, so to speak, and prepares to depart.

She does not carry as much luggage as the Queen of England carries when she goes from Buckingham Palace to the Isle of Wight.

She merely gathers up her thousands of eyes, her shortish, but still valuable tongue, her basketless legs, and other personal possessions and starts off, taking with her most of the old bees in the hive, and leaving behind the young queen with the young bees

94

and the honey-comb, and the brood comb full of eggs and larvæ and pupæ.

She is very generous to the young queen, who of course is her own daughter, and leaves all the furniture and silver spoons and everything of that sort behind.

Away she goes, with her faithful followers surrounding her in a dense swarm.

The whole swarm goes careering through the air like a small cyclone, and I for one should not like to stand in its path.

Some say the bees send out scouts to find a good place before the swarm starts, either a hollow tree or some other convenient shelter, or else they go into a nice new hive if somebody has been watching and has one ready.

Into the new home they go, and to work they go; and in a little while you would never suspect the family had recently moved in, so busy and so thoroughly at home do they all appear.

They build new combs, make new honey and beebread, and just as soon as the cells are ready the queen continues her egg-laying.

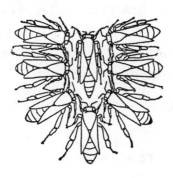

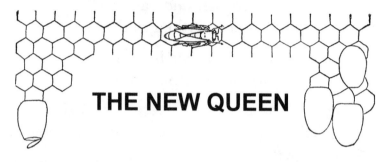

THE NEW QUEEN

MEANTIME all is not fair weather in the old hive.

The new queen, although just out of her cell, understands her business perfectly, and is quite capable of going about it, but there are complications. Hers was not the only queen cell in that hive.

There were others. And now, just as she has ascended the throne with the old queen peaceably out of the way, the succession being accomplished without opposition, lo and behold! she hears a sound,—a sound that probably sends the blood to her heart, and causes her very toes to tingle.

The sound she hears is not that of cannon afar, nor of drum-beats in the distance, but it might as well be, for it is the piping of another young queen just about to come forth from its cell.

The throne is not secure, after all, for there is another queen to dispute it.

Of course there are ways of disposing of rivals to

the throne, or there used to be, as any one who has read the early history of England knows.

You may smother them in a tower, or poison them, or do something of that sort.

Bees know how to smother bees that they hate, and they know how to poison them, but queen bees prefer to fight like queens for their thrones, and not get them by stealth or by striking in the dark: that is, if the rival is already out of her cradle.

If a second queen hatches out of her cell before the first young queen finds her, there is a fight.

What do I see? I must go over and fight her!

Come on, I am ready for you!

The workers stand around and watch the conflict, but they never interfere, nor have I ever heard that they take sides and cheer their own candidate.

The combatants seize each other with their jaws, and clasp each other with their feet, trying in every way to thrust the fatal poisoned dagger into a vital part,—that is, into the soft parts between the rings of the abdomen, or where the neck joins the thorax, or the thorax the abdomen,—all these places being soft and allowing a dagger that is thrust into them to reach the inner vital parts.

At length the fatal thrust is given: one of the queens is victor; the other lies dead upon the field of battle.

The workers carry out the dead body, but whether they mourn I cannot say. Certainly they do not have a grand funeral. I suppose it would not be exactly polite to the victorious queen to show too much sorrow for the vanquished one.

Evidently our queen considers one such display of courage quite enough to establish her royal character, for she does not waste time fighting any more queens, but goes to the remaining queen cells, pulls off the caps where the bottled-up queen babies lie, and sticks her dagger right into their poor, soft, helpless little bodies.

After she has stung all the baby queens she puts up her dagger, very likely determined never to put anything so valuable to such a use again, for you remember her sting is also her ovipositor.

She does not lose it when she stings a bee, because the parts where the sting enters are so soft that she can pull it out again; but you can imagine what a sad wound the barbs make when pulled out.

Workers never sting a queen. If a strange queen is put into the hive, or flies in by mistake, and they do not want her, they gather about her so closely as to smother her to death, but they will not sting her.

Only queens sting queens.

If there should happen to be a good many bees still in the hive after a swarm leaves, the workers will not allow the queens to fight, but surround them and keep them apart until the older queen can be sent off with another swarm.

If the hive is very much crowded, the bees may swarm out of it several times in one season.

When all is serene within the hive, if the day is fair, the young queen takes an airing.

She does not have an escort, but goes alone to view the beautiful world outside the hive.

Huber was the first to discover that she flies up into the blue sky, where she meets a drone, who is her mate. He fills her pocket, which she carries on purpose, with pollen, not flower-pollen, but bee-pollen. This pollen lasts as long as she lives, and she uses it to fertilize the queen and worker eggs.

So you see the drone is not so useless as he seems. Indeed, if it were not for him, there could be no workers and no queens.

When she has taken her airing, Queen Apis goes home, and she never leaves the hive alone again. In fact, she never leaves it at all, except at the end, when she goes off with a swarm.

As the season wears on, the workers take counsel together. Winter is coming, and what *will* become of them all if the supplies give out?

There must be no more mouths to feed than necessary. The queen, of course, must be taken care of, and so must the workers; but there are the drones, perhaps hundreds or even thousands of them. They are no longer of any use: they bring in no honey; they do no work; they only endanger the lives of the whole family by eating up the winter food, so these little brown workers, on the plea of necessity, send the drones to the happy hunting grounds.

Whether they are sorry about it or not I do not know; but, in any event, they fall upon their poor brothers and sting them to death, or else drive them from the hive, where they soon die from cold, exposure, and hunger.

In late summer you sill sometimes see a disconsolate drone sitting on a flower, very likely grieving at the bitterness of his lot.

Miss Apis, it seems to us very cruel of you to treat your brothers so.

But we must remember that bees are not people, and that what would be very wicked in us may be perfectly right in them.

The worker-bees labor very hard through the summer, so that sometimes they wear themselves out in a few weeks, and die.

A disconsolate drone

Those hatched later in the season live through the winter, and are all ready to begin work as soon as the flowers come in the spring.

Bees spend the winter clustered together in the hive,

and are then so inactive that they seem to be scarcely alive.

When bees go out from the hive for the first time to gather nectar, they are very smooth and fine-looking.

But they, too, grow old. Their pretty velvety down wears off, and their wings become broken and ragged. I do not think they turn grey or get wrinkles in their faces, but they certainly do get to wear very shabby looking wings.

A Veteran

FANCIES AND FACTS
ABOUT BEES

P EOPLE used to think the queen-bee was a king, and ruled over all the bees in the hive.

They thought a hive of bees was a little kingdom, with an army, and officers, and all sorts of workers.

Huckle-
berries

When you get old enough to read Shakespeare's "Henry V.," you will find in it a pretty story about the bees. He says, "They have a king, and officers of sorts;" and tells how some of the bees act as magistrates at home, while other go abroad to trade like merchants, and still others are armed soldiers. Some, he tells us, are masons, and do the building, others make the bread and honey, yet others are porters and carry heavy burdens, while the judge hands the drones over to be executed.

We know the truth about bees now, and yet we like to read these old stories.

It used to be thought that bees carried little stones in their feet on windy days, so as not to be blown away. Probably the people saw their pollen balls and mistook them for ballast.

They used to think, too, that when the bees were belated and had to stay out all night, they would lie on their backs to keep their wings dry.

A good many people, even yet, will not sell bees, because they think it is unlucky; and when bees swarm, they sometimes use charms to keep them from going away. An old German bee-keeper, who lived in the United States, had such a charm.

He told it to a little girl, but said it would bring bad luck if she were to repeat it to another girl. She might tell it to a man, or a boy, and he to another girl, and so on, but a girl must never tell it to a girl, nor a boy to a boy. I will give you the charm in German, for those of you who understand German.

When you see the bees swarming, you must say to them,—

Liebe Bienen, und liebe Bienen Mutter,
Setzt euch auf Rasen und grünes Gras.
Im Namen des Vaters,
        des Sohnes, und des Heiligen Geistes.
                AMEN.

You see, it is really a little prayer to the bees, and this is the English translation:—

Dear bees, and dear mother of the bees,
Place yourselves upon the meadow
    and the green grass,
In the name of the Father, and the Son,
    and the Holy Ghost.

AMEN.

A good many still think the bees must be told when there is a death in the family, or else they will go away.

A member of the family goes at night and knocks on the hives, and says, "So-and-so is dead," and sometimes adds a little prayer to the bees not to leave. Sometime a piece of black ribbon or crape is tied on the hives.

Whittier has written a beautiful poem called, "Telling the Bees," which I hope you will read.

The ancients used to believe that the bee was given its marvellous habits by Jupiter, the king of the gods, because the bees fed him with honey when he was a baby and lay concealed in a cave, while his angry father searched for him.

It seems that the gods had their troubles as well as human beings in those days, and Jupiter's father, Saturn, who was king, was very much afraid of his own children.

An oracle had told him that they would displace him;

so he settled the matter, as he thought, by swallowing them as soon as they were born.

This unfortunate habit greatly distressed Saturn's wife, Rhea, and when Jupiter was born she gave him to the care of the Curetes,—a Cretan tribe who were very true to their charge.

They used to dance about the young god and drown his cries by rattling bronze weapons, so that Saturn might not hear and so find the royal infant. Jupiter was fed upon milk and honey by the goat Amalthea and the bees. This is the end of the story, so far as bees are concerned, but perhaps you will be glad to know that when Jupiter grew up he married Metis, whom we would call Prudence, and she administered a draught to Father Saturn, which caused him to disgorge all his children. Then Jupiter and his disgorged brothers, Neptune and Pluto, made true the words of the oracle by dethroning their very unfatherly father, and dividing his kingdom among them. Jupiter took the heavens for his portion, as you know, while Neptune took the sea, and Pluto the underground world, or the realms of the dead.

A great many people think that when bees are about to swarm, a loud noise will prevent them from leaving, and they clash on tin pans, or ring bells, or blow whistles, or do anything they can think of to make a hullabaloo. No doubt they sometimes equal the uproar made by the Curetes about the infant Jupiter.

Honey was very highly valued in ancient Greece and Italy, and that which came from Mount Hymettus was specially prized. Hymettus is a mountain in Greece, near Athens, and used to contain famous bee-pastures.

A bee-pasture, you know, is a place grown over with flowers; and Mount Hymettus was said to be rosy-purple, it was so covered with heather blossoms.

Hybla, an ancient city on the sea-coast in Sicily, was also very celebrated for its honey.

Probably the best bee-pastures in the world, to-day, are in California. A great deal of the honey is made there.

Honey is not valued as highly as it used to be, because we now have sugar. But you can imagine that before the sugar-cane was cultivated, and when people had no sweet but honey, it was a most important and valuable article of food.

Honey is very good for children and for old people. It is more digestible than sugar, and most children like it better.

You remember how "The queen was in the parlor eating bread and honey," and I think it was a very good occupation for a queen or for anybody else.

A great deal of poetry has been written about bees, and there is one little verse that everybody knows. It was written by Dr. Watts.

"How doth the little honey bee
    Improve each shining hour,
And gather honey all the day
    From every opening flower."

The most interesting thing we have learned in modern times about bees is their relation to the flowers. Some plants cannot set seeds at all without the help of the bees, and they are very great helpers in gardens and orchards.

If you want your trees loaded with apples and pears, be sure to put a bee-hive near the orchard.

Near Boston, where a great many cucumbers are raised for market in the winter in glass houses, hives of bees are kept in the houses to fertilize the cucumbers. If the little bees did not go from flower to flower carrying the pollen from one to another, a large force of men would have to be employed to brush the pistil of each cucumber blossom with pollen.

Wild Cherry

BOMBUS, THE BUMBLE-BEE

A PIS MELLIFICA is not the only honey-bee in this country.

Indeed, she is not even a native of America, but was brought over from Europe more than two hundred years ago.

The bumble-bees, like the Indians, belong to America. They were here when Columbus discovered the New World.

There are a great many bumble-bees in different parts of the world, and more than sixty species in North America. The habits of them all are very much alike, however,

Red Clover

108

so if we make the acquaintance of one, we shall know something of all.

The bumble-bees do not live in hives, and they do not store up honey in beautiful waxen combs.

Generally they have a nest in the ground, though sometimes they choose a woodpile, or other convenient place.

Bumble-bee nests are often found in haying time. When the grass is being cut the horses step on the nests, when out fly the angry bees and sting the horses and the men and boys.

Sometimes there are so many bees' nests in a meadow that it is difficult to get the hay.

Madam Bombus makes her nest in a hollow in the ground under a tuft of grass, and it is so near the surface that one could easily dig it out with the fingers, if it were not for Madam Bombus herself.

Put your fingers into her nest and see what she will do.

She will sting you on the nose for one thing. She seems fond of stinging people on the nose.

Queen Bombus does not have a whole hive full of workers to help her when she starts her nest.

On the contrary, the workers and drones die in the fall, and the queen is left all alone. She crawls into some snug corner and sleeps through the winter. When spring comes she wakes up, stretches herself, smells the early flowers, feels the warm sun, and away she flies. She first goes in search of a home.

You can see her in the springtime flying about, hunting carefully for a good place to make her nest.

When she has found a home that suits her, she goes to the flowers and gathers pollen.

From morning until night she works as hard as she can tugging large balls of pollen to her hole in the ground.

What do you think she does with it? She has no waxen cells to store it away in, so she just piles it together in her nest.

In this mass of pollen she lays her eggs. She always lays fertilized eggs early in the season; but I suppose she does not feed the young bees very generously on bee-milk, so they hatch into workers instead of queens.

Of course this is just what she wants. As soon as the workers begin to come out, she can stay at home and let them gather the pollen.

My Bombus

The bombus is covered all over with hair, as you know, and has bands of yellow and black hairs across her body.

The bombus that I know best has a yellow jacket, and a broad yellow band across the top of her abdomen.

The tail-end of her abdomen is black. She is a very

pretty, furry bee, and like all the bombuses, her wings are dark brown in color.

The honey-bee's wings are as clear as glass, and that is one way you can tell a honey-bee from a bumble-bee.

Well, Madam Bombus lays her eggs in the mass of pollen, and they hatch into little larvæ, like those of the honey-bees, only not so small.

You see, Madam Bombus has to do all the work herself; so, I suppose it saves trouble to have the infants cradled in good pollen, so they can help themselves without troubling their mother. She feeds them on bee-milk at first; but later, I suspect, they have to eat their cradles.

They grow fast; no doubt they eat a great deal of pollen.

When it comes time for them to change into pupæ, what do you suppose happens? I do not believe you could guess if you tried a month.

You see, they have no wax cells in which they can be bottled up.

Queen Bombus does not cap them over, as the honey-bees do, and

leave them to their fate. She cannot bottle up her babies, because she has no bottles.

I shall have to tell you the secret.

They bottle themselves up! You remember how the Apis baby, in its pretty waxen cell, spun a silk nightcap when it was capped over? Baby Bombus spins a whole nightgown.

She eats a hole in the pollen about her, large enough to lie in comfortably, then she begins to spin, and does not stop until she has made for herself a yellow cocoon. It looks a little like the cocoon of a silkworm, only it is much darker in color, and the lower part is embedded in pollen. The upper part is sometimes quite clean and pretty.

I looked into the nest of the bombus with a yellow jacket and a yellow band across the upper end of her abdomen, and this is what I saw. Just a pile of cocoons, you see. In each cocoon is a bee-baby.

The larva lies curled up in its cocoon with its head bent over, as you can see in this next picture.

 But in a few days it changes into a pupa. The young pupa is very pretty and it deserves its name. You know *pupa* means doll; and if the pupa, when first formed, does not look like a bee-doll, I do not know what it does look like.

I will try to draw you some pictures of these pupæ, though no pictures can do them justice. They are as white as snow, and sometimes have pink eyes, though sometimes their eyes are blue. They look as if they had been very beautifully carved from white ivory. You can see their little buds of wings held close to their sides, and their long white tongues down in front, and their pretty snow-white legs cuddled up close to their bodies, so as not to take up too much room.

Honey-bee pupæ are as pretty as these, but they are smaller and not so easily seen.

Soon these pretty white "dolls" become darker in color, and soft hairs begin to appear. Then their wings enlarge, the down has covered their bodies, their legs are strong and black, they are no longer "dolls," but are perfect bees and are ready to come out.

All they have to do, is bite a hole in the end of their cocoons, and step out. They are damp at first, and their hairs cling to their bodies; but soon they are dry and fuzzy and as handsome as young bees ought to be.

When the bees first come out, their jackets and the upper part of their abdomens are white instead of yellow.

I suppose they are tow-headed in infancy, like some other young people you and I know. But their white, baby hairs soon turn to a bright canary yellow, and in two or three days they would probably sting you if you called them "babies."

The worker-bees are only half as large as the queens, though they vary a good deal in size. Sometimes the eggs laid in corners, or under the large cocoons, hatch into poor little larvæ, that have no chance to grow. So they make tiny little cocoons, and hatch out into funny little bits of bumble-bees. Sometimes these little dwarfs are no larger than honey-bees. But, I can tell you, they feel as big as anybody. They buzz about and gather pollen and honey like the other bees.

A Dwarf

Late in the summer Queen Bombus lays fertilized eggs that make queens. I suppose the larvæ are fed on all the bee-milk they want, and so become queens instead of workers. Queen Bombus, also, toward the end of the summer lays unfertilized eggs, and of course these hatch into drones.

Bumble-bee queens do not kill each other, and the bumble-bees do not kill their drones.

After the queens and drones are hatched, they mate high in the air, and the queen stores away the pollen of the drone until next spring.

When the cold weather comes, the drones and workers die, and the queen hides away.

Some bumble-bees store up honey in the empty cocoons after the young bees have left them, but you can imagine it is not very good honey. Some bumble-bees make wax and use it to finish out the cocoons into better cells, or even to make a few coarse cells, or to mat together the grass over the nest to keep the rain out. But my bumble-bees had no wax at all in their nest, and at the time I saw it they had not stored away any honey.

The Bombus family is very small compared to the

Apis family, for sometimes there will be only a dozen bees in a nest, again there will be several dozen.

Bumble-bees are very good play-fellows. If you want to have a good time watching the bees, catch one or two large bumble-bees in a net and let them loose on the window. They will not sting you unless you touch them. Even if they get on you, if you keep perfectly still they will leave without hurting you.

You can give your pet bombus a drop of honey, or a little sugar and water, and see its long brown tongue lick it up.

If you want to see it perform its toilet, you can breathe upon it gently.

This makes it very angry, and it will buzz with its wings for a moment, then go to work to clean itself all over.

Bumble-bees have a funny way of sticking out their legs at you, as if they meant to strike you. When you come near one, out fly its legs in quite a threatening manner.

Honey-bees do this too, but not so much as bumble-bees.

The very best place to watch bees is in the fields.

If you sit down near a nice patch of red clover, you will be very sure to meet a bombus before long.

She will not disturb you, and you can get as close

to her as you please, so long as you do not touch her. You can watch her put her tongue into the little clover tubes. She is very fond of red clover, and she can get its honey, but the honey-bee cannot, because the clover tube is too long for Miss Apis's tongue. The red clover depends upon the bumble-bee for fertilization, and an interesting story is told of how clover was introduced into Australia.

There was no red clover in Australia until the white settlers took the seed there and sowed it. Then the clover grew, but bore no seed, so of course it did not amount to much. People said, what is the matter with the clover; why will it not go to seed?

I wonder if you could have told them? Finally somebody told of the relation between the bumble-bees and the clover, and said the clover needed the bees,—for there were no bumble-bees in Australia. So some nest of bumble-bees were taken to Australia, and the clover then bore seeds.

I once had a bumble-bee that did not know how to get nectar from red clover.

It was hatched in my room, and fed on sugar and water for several days.

Then it was given some clover, but it seemed to be

too old to learn. It wanted the nectar, for evidently it smelled it, and tried to get it, but it could not find the openings into the flower tubes.

It was very funny to see poor Miss Bombus run her tongue along the *outside* of the little flowers that make up the clover head. She found the opening to one or two of them finally, but she never became an expert at gathering clover nectar. You see, she began to practise too late in life.

You will sometimes see bumble-bees asleep on the flowers toward night. Perhaps they have wandered too far from home; perhaps they think flower petals make a very dainty bedroom. Often the bees kept in a room will take a nap on a cloudy day.

You can tell when a bee is asleep, because it *looks* as if it were asleep.

It does not shut its eyes, of course, but it looks very droopy and sleepy.

Look at that bee on the iris bud; wouldn't you *know* it had gone to sleep?

You can get a great deal of pleasure from the bees by watching them out of doors. You can see them go into different kinds of flowers and find out just how they take the nectar.

Bees never sting unless you go too near their hives or else touch them. You can watch the bees out of doors and in your room as much as you please without the slightest danger.

You can keep bees in the house and feed them on different kinds of flowers. They have to learn how to get the nectar from a new kind of flower. They will try and try until they have found the right opening.

When once they have learned their way into a flower, they can usually go at once to the nectar in another flower of the same kind.

You see, they experiment until they find out what to do, and then they remember.

CPSIA information can be obtained
at www.ICGtesting.com
Printed in the USA
BVHW07s1740200718
522054BV00002B/94/P

9 781599 153186